by Dr. Randy T. Johnson

WITH CONTRIBUTIONS BY:

NOBLE BAIRD
JOHN CARTER
JAMES CLOUSE
CALEB COMBS
CAROLE COMBS
ISAIAH COMBS
JEN COMBS
SIERRA COMBS
BRETT EBERLE
DONNA FOX
DEBBIE GABBARA
RICHIE HENSON
JOHN HUBBARD
DEBBIE KERR

CHUCK LINDSEY
LORNA LYMAN
JAMES MANN
WES MCCULLOUGH
MARK O'CONNOR
JILL OSMON
KEN PERRY
PHILIP PIASECKI
MAX SINCLAIR
RYAN STORY
KYLE WENDEL
KATRINA YOUNG
TOMMY YOUNGQUIST

DESIGNED BY: CASEY MAXWELL
FORMATTED BY: SHAWNA JOHNSON

Copyright © 2018 The River Church

All rights reserved. No part of this book may be reproduced or transmitted in any form or by any means, electronic or mechanical, including photocopying, recording or by any information storage and retrieval system, without the written permission of The River Church. Inquiries should be sent to the publisher.

First Edition, February 2018

Published by:
The River Church
8393 E. Holly Rd.
Holly, MI 48442

Scriptures are taken from the Bible,
English Standard Version (ESV)

THE RIVER CHURCH

Printed in the United States of America

CONTENTS

WEEK 1
DELIVERY ON TIME

09   Study Guide

15   Devotion 1: Timing is Everything

17   Devotion 2: Anointed One

19   Devotion 3: Jesus is Never Late

21   Devotion 4: Perfect Timing

23   Devotion 5: On Time Delivery

25   Devotion 6: No Ledge

WEEK 2
DELIVERY STATUS

29   Study Guide

37   Devotion 1: Sin

39   Devotion 2: Satan's Family

41   Devotion 3: Hell

43   Devotion 4: Wrath of God

45   Devotion 5: Self

47   Devotion 6: Chains

WEEK 3
DELIVERY MAN

51   Study Guide

57   Devotion 1: Joseph

61   Devotion 2: Moses

63   Devotion 3: Joshua

65   Devotion 4: Boaz

67   Devotion 5: Gideon

69   Devotion 6: David

WEEK 4
DELIVERY PLAN

73   Study Guide

81   Devotion 1: Judas

83   Devotion 2: Pilate

85   Devotion 3: Religious Leaders

87   Devotion 4: Caiaphas

89   Devotion 5: Roman Soldiers

91   Devotion 6: Barabbas

WEEK 5

DELIVERY DAY

95 Study Guide

105 Devotion 1: The Resurrection

107 Devotion 2: He is Not Here

109 Devotion 3: Victory

111 Devotion 4: Celebrate

113 Devotion 5: Special Occasions with Grandma Eddie

115 Devotion 6: G.R.A.C.E.

PREFACE

What does it mean to be delivered?

The word "delivered" is frequently associated with sending or mailing a package. Some of the key elements include: making sure the delivery is on time, checking the delivery status, having a reliable delivery man, choosing a company that has a proven delivery plan, and finally a delivery day. All of these elements are examined and compared through the lenses of Jesus' mission.

Delivered consists of five study guides for personal or group discussion and thirty devotions to help you realize and appreciate that Jesus did everything necessary for you to be "delivered" from death to life.

01

DELIVERY ON TIME

CHUCK LINDSEY,
REACH PASTOR

DELIVERY ON TIME WEEK 1

"*H*im, being delivered by the determined purpose and foreknowledge of God, you have taken by lawless hands, have crucified, and put to death."
Acts 2:23 (NKJV)

Every parent understands the concept of a "due date." It is the date a doctor gives to an excited couple who is asking for the date their baby will be born. Every parent also understands that this "due date" is, at best, a guess, an estimate. Research proves that this is true as reports indicate that less than 5% of babies are ever born on their actual due date. That does not stop doctors from giving due dates, and it does not stop expectant couples from hoping in them.

How far before or beyond your due date were your child(ren) born?
_____
_____

Imagine something with me for a moment. What if, on your twentieth birthday, you were given a very old diary. In that diary, you see written the date, time, and place of your birth. Below that, you find your full name, your hair color, eye color, birth weight, and birth length. As you turn the page, you see the names and descriptions of your parents and siblings. Another page turn tells about the things you did as a baby, then as a toddler, and then as a child. Another turn reminds you of key moments in your life; places you have been, cities in which you have lived, and people you have known. Another page describes in detail your character, the person you are. It tells of the things you have said and done as a teenager. Then, you notice something interesting; the diary does not stop at your present age. There are more pages. It describes where you will go to school, who you will marry, and where you will work. It is not generalities; it is specific. It is written as though it had already happened. In wonder, you read of each of your children, their names, their personalities,

DELIVERY ON TIME WEEK 1

who they marry, their children, and their homes. Then finally you read of how you will pass into eternity.

Surprise, you find out that the whole diary was written 700 years before you were ever born!

What would this mean?
_____
_____
_____

Who could have written such a diary about your life?
_____
_____
_____

If the details of your life up to this point, written 700 years before, were accurate down to the smallest details, what would that mean for all that is written after it?
_____
_____
_____

This is what the coming of Jesus Christ was. His birth date, time (Malachi 3:1), place (Micah 5:2; Hosea 11:1), and circumstances (virgin birth - Genesis 3:15; Isaiah 7:14) were all written out in incredible detail, hundreds of years before He came. The specifics of His life were spelled out, not in generalities, but as though they had already occurred. Hundreds of years before He arrived, we read of "who" He would be (Genesis 12:3) and what He would do (Jeremiah 23:5). We read of His life and ministry (Zechariah 9:9). We read of His suffering and death (Jeremiah 31:15; Psalm 41:9; Zechariah 11:12; Daniel 9:26; Isaiah 53; Psalm 22:1, 8, 18; Exodus 12:46). We read of His resurrection and life forever (Psalm 16:8-11; Isaiah 53:10-11; Psalm 68:18; Psalm 110:1). We also read of why He came and what it means for us. All of this was written out for us, hundreds of years before He came, in a diary, if you will, called the Bible.

The biblical term for this is called "prophecy," and it is the special ability of God alone. Man has tried to predict the future over and over and has failed miserably. People like Nostradamus are often cited as "prophets," but when you examine their "prophesies," you find that they are nothing more than "due date" guesses. Their "prophesies" are general and obscure rather than detailed and clear. It is only the Bible, indeed the God of the Bible, who operates outside of time and space, who writes out the details of events and times with clarity and mind-blowing specificity.

One such occasion is found in a prophecy given to Daniel, the prophet of God. In the ninth chapter of his book, he writes these incredible words:

"Know therefore and understand, that from the going forth of the command to restore and build Jerusalem until Messiah the Prince, there shall be seven weeks and sixty-two weeks; the street shall be built again, and the wall, even in troublesome times. And after the sixty-two weeks Messiah shall be cut off, but not for Himself; and the people of the prince who is to come shall destroy the city and the sanctuary. The end of it shall be with a flood, and till the end of the war desolations are determined." Daniel 9:25-26 (NKJV)

Maybe you have read this before; maybe you have not. If you have read it, maybe it made sense, maybe it did not. Maybe you thought someone was speaking a different language and just moved on to the next verses? This passage is incredibly important. It is a

DELIVERY ON TIME WEEK 1

prophecy. It is a "due date" if you will. It tells when the Messiah, the Savior of the world would come. Let us look at it a little deeper.

The first thing we have to understand is that at the time this prophecy was given, Jerusalem was in ruins. Most of God's people (the Hebrews) were in the nation of Babylon. They had been carried off captive from Israel to Babylon during three waves of capture. Daniel was among the first group taken to Babylon. The prophecy says that a *"command"* will be given, by someone in authority, to *"rebuild Jerusalem"* (again currently in ruins). The prophecy says that when that *"command"* is given it begins a countdown. This countdown would end with the coming of the promised Savior, the Messiah of God. The coming of the One who would finally crush the head of the serpent (Genesis 3:15) and restore what had been lost through sin.

So it says, that from the giving of the *"command to restore and build Jerusalem"* until the coming of *"Messiah the Prince"* there will be *"seven weeks and sixty-two weeks."* What does that mean? A *"week"* here refers to not seven days, but seven years. So, one week would be seven years. So we see 62 weeks (62 x 7 years = 434 years) and seven weeks (7 x 7 years = 49 years) for a total of 69 weeks or 483 total years. Have I lost you yet? Great! To put it simply, from the time the command is given to rebuild Jerusalem until the Messiah comes will be 483 years. That is pretty specific is it not? Nothing vague or fuzzy about it. There would be 483 years until the long-awaited promised Savior comes.

The promise continues in a few years. On March 5, 444 B.C. Persian ruler Artaxerxes Longimanus issued a decree allowing the Jews to rebuild the walls of Jerusalem. It was a command given from the Persian king protecting the Hebrew people, allowing them to finally rebuild their beloved city. From that moment the clock began to tick.

The countdown began. Now, I am sure all the math wizards reading this already have it figured. For those of us that were not so gifted, when you add 483 years to March 5, 444 B.C. and you take into account that the Hebrew calendar (Gregorian calendar) consisted of 360 days (rather than 365) it brings you down to March 30, A.D. 33. It is the day that Jesus rode into Jerusalem on a donkey to the shouts and singing of the multitudes saying **"Hosanna! Save us now!"** Although it would be just a couple of days until He would die on that cross for our sins, this moment, this joyful moment, was what Daniel foretold. **"Messiah the Prince"** had come. The Savior of the world had come, just as God said He would and at "just the right time." His "due date" was perfectly accurate and He arrived "on time."

DELIVERY ON TIME WEEK 1

TIMING IS EVERYTHING

DELIVERY ON TIME, DEVOTION 1
Ken Perry

I am a fan of history. I get it from my father, I am sure. It was my favorite subject in school as well. Unfortunately, I think its lessons and importance are somewhat lost on the younger generation. It is well said that those who do not learn from it, will repeat it and we can see the fallout of that today. I enjoy the period of the Civil War and look forward to the time when I can travel to cities such as Boston, Cambridge, and Philadelphia to soak in the rich history, if those evidences still exist, that formed our great nation. One such story is of a herald of sorts whose name is Paul Revere. Popularized in Henry Wadsworth Longfellow's 1863 poem, *The Midnight Ride of Paul Revere*, we see a loyal patriot risk his life to warn the colonial militia of the impending invasion of the British troops. He was also instrumental in forming an early warning system so effective that people in towns twenty-five miles away knew of the Army's movements while they were still unloading the boats in Cambridge Harbor. Although he is wrongly credited with saying, "The British are Coming" (he actually said, "the regulars are coming out"), it is important to note that an alarm raised by three riders allowed the Patriots to push the British troops back to the Harbor. Think about it, all that without GPS and iPhones. It goes beyond saying that timing was indeed everything.

The Bible is not just history; it is the present and future telling of His-story. In Isaiah 40, Isaiah is speaking to the Israelites as yet future exiles. As David Jeremiah states in his commentary, "God still cares for them and intends to deliver them...and renew their broken covenant relationship. To facilitate reconciliation, God announces that He will send His Suffering Servant to atone for their sins." In verses 3-5 we read of another Herald, **"A voice cries: 'In the wilderness prepare the way of the Lord; make straight in the desert a highway for our God. Every valley shall be lifted up, and every mountain and hill be made low; the uneven ground shall become level, and the rough places a plain. And the glory of the Lord shall be revealed, and all flesh shall see it together, for the**

DELIVERY ON TIME DEVOTION 1

mouth of the Lord has spoken.'" He alludes to the custom of a prince that would send men before him to prepare the way in which they were planning to pass. It is a prophetic warning of the perfect timing of the coming of our Lord seven hundred years later. God's people had a broken relationship with Him. Separation was caused by sin. Through Isaiah, God was calling them to repentance, leading to reconciliation, resulting in a relationship.

Is that what God is calling you to today? Are there impassable paths that need to be made straight in your life? Are there hills and valleys that need to be leveled? Call on the one true God that sent His Son, at the perfect time in His-story, to reclaim that which was lost in the garden. Claim for yourself that which was won on Calvary, a new beginning of a reconciled friend.

The timing is perfect, and the time is now.

ANOINTED ONE

DELIVERY ON TIME, DEVOTION 2
Noble Baird // *Community Center Director*

All throughout middle school and high school, one of my favorite subjects was math. I just always loved solving different problems, trying to find points on a graph, and of course being able to use the massive TI calculator! No matter how much I did enjoy math class, I did not always solve the problem correctly. There would be times where I thought I rocked a test, only to find out that because I had divided or subtracted one number incorrectly, I got the whole equation wrong. Needless to say, I soon figured out that although I enjoyed math class, it was not the career for me to pursue!

As we take a look at God's Word, we find math spread throughout it. From Genesis chapter 1 through Revelation chapter 22, God is always using math to speak to us. One of the most fascinating and honestly more difficult equations for me to follow along with is found in Daniel 9:24-27. Here, we have the prophet Daniel writing about the coming of Christ. Starting in verse 24 he writes, **"Seventy weeks are decreed about your people and your holy city, to finish the transgression, to put an end to sin, and to atone for iniquity, to bring in everlasting righteousness, to seal both vision and prophet, and to anoint a most holy place. Know therefore and understand that from the going out of the word to restore and build Jerusalem to the coming of an anointed one, a prince, there shall be seven weeks. Then for sixty-two weeks it shall be built again with squares and moat, but in a troubled time. And after the sixty-two weeks, an anointed one shall be cut off and shall have nothing."** So, what we have is an amazing equation from Daniel, predicting Christ's coming and His death on the cross. Daniel writes about the "anointed one" or in other words the Messiah, who we know as Jesus.

Daniel gave this prophecy over 700 years before the birth of Christ. However, following along the timeline after the destruction of Jerusalem and the rule of the Persian emperor Artaxerxes, Daniel

DELIVERY ON TIME DEVOTION 2

gives us the exact years leading to Christ's death on the cross. One of the things I love about this passage is that this is the only time in the Old Testament that Christ is referred to as the ***"anointed one."*** Thousands of years ago, Daniel knew about the Easter season we would celebrate. He knew that the Anointed One was going to come and mend that broken relationship between a fallen world and a just God. So, as you continue in your week, remember the Anointed One whom Daniel prophesied about will return.

JESUS IS NEVER LATE

DELIVERY ON TIME, DEVOTION 3
Philip Piasecki // *Worship Leader*

The concept of a due date has always been fascinating to me. When Mary and I found out she was pregnant with our daughter Molly, we immediately wanted to know a due date. At the first couple doctor appointments, the number jumped around a bit, and it finally settled on April 15th. April 15th we could bank on meeting our new baby girl, or at least that is what we thought. April 15th came and went with no baby. Mary had already been done with work for a month, and I had taken that week off of work to be prepared all because of the due date. Every day after the due date passed was filled with stress and anxiety. Every text or call I received from Mary, I assumed would be telling me that she had gone into labor. It took another twelve days past her "due date" before labor began, and another full day before Molly was born. Altogether, she came thirteen days past her due date. We waited and waited for her, and then had to wait just a little bit longer. Throughout this whole time, I could not help but think about the Jewish people waiting for the arrival of Jesus. They had been promised a Messiah, and it was up to them to wait patiently for Him to arrive. Not only was the arrival of Jesus' prophesied, but specific aspects of His birth, life, death, and resurrection were foretold in the Old Testament as well. Jesus, without fail, fulfilled every one of those prophecies!

Take time today and read through Isaiah chapter 53. The whole chapter is prophecy about Jesus' life, and He fulfilled them all. It gives details about how Jesus would be killed; it is a sobering reminder of how truly brutal the death of Christ was. While reading through these prophecies that Christ fulfilled, I kept thinking "Jesus is never late." His arrival to earth, ministry, death, and resurrection were all done in His perfect timing. No matter what is going on in your own life, Jesus is never late. His timing is perfect in all things; it is up to us to fully trust Him through the circumstances of life. Easter is an incredible reminder that Jesus was delivered over to death, to deliver us from eternal punishment. When we give our lives to Christ, His Holy Spirit then lives inside of us, guiding and sustaining

DELIVERY ON TIME DEVOTION 3

us every day. Jesus is always there for us; do not despair if you feel like He is not close. It is so natural for us to think our circumstances are never going to change, or the difficulty we are facing is never going to end. I have gone through difficulties where I felt like God was never going to show up and intervene, then in hindsight, I was able to see how He was present throughout the entire situation. Jesus loves you, cares for you, and will never forsake you.

Jesus is never late!

PERFECT TIMING

DELIVERY ON TIME, DEVOTION 4

Debbie Gabbara // *Assistant to the Gathering Pastor*

Are you a good waiter? You know, are you good at waiting for something?

How do you wait for news, something to happen, something to be delivered, or something exciting that is coming up? Do you wait patiently? Do you get weary in the waiting? Do you wait expectantly? Are you a complainer, or do you just wait quietly? You might be one who tells everyone why you are waiting!

Imagine you have heard about something, heard about it your whole life. It is something your parents told you about it, your grandparents told them about it, and everyone around you knew about it. The Lord was sending One who would save His people, but no one knew exactly whom it was or when He would come. The prophets said the Messiah was coming. Over the years, God provided in miraculous ways and showed His people mercy and faithfulness, and some waited with expectation for the fulfillment of God's Word. However, time kept moving, and no one came. Their faith faded, and most forgot God's promises.

More than 700 years passed after Isaiah prophesied that the Lord would send a sign, **"Behold, the virgin shall conceive and bear a son, and shall call his name Immanuel"** (Isaiah 7:14). In the Gospel of Matthew, that prophecy was fulfilled when the Lord told Joseph in a dream that Mary would bear a son and call His name Jesus.

The prophet, Micah, prophesied that the Messiah would be born in Bethlehem.

"But you, O Bethlehem Ephrathah, who are too little to be among the clans of Judah, from you shall come forth for me one who is to be ruler in Israel, whose coming forth is from of old, from ancient days" (Micah 5:2).

DELIVERY ON TIME DEVOTION 4

Mary and Joseph did not live in Bethlehem Ephrathah, the city of David, but because God's timing is always perfect, that is where they were when the time came that Mary, the virgin, would deliver her child, Jesus the Son of God.

Galatians 4:4-5 says, **"But when the fullness of time had come, God sent forth his Son, born of woman, born under the law, to redeem those who were under the law, so that we might receive adoption as sons."**

It was the **"fullness of time,"** timing that was perfectly and meticulously planned by God. Prophecies that were given hundreds of years before were perfectly fulfilled in God's timing.

Jesus is the One for whom they were waiting. He came to save us all. In God's perfect time Jesus died on the cross, conquered death, and rose again.

Prophecy also tells us that Jesus the Christ will come again. Jesus said that He has gone to prepare a place for us. We talk about it with others, we tell our children about it, and our grandparents told us about it. Expectantly, in faith, we tell others of His love while we wait.

Will you be ready when Jesus comes again? The Bible tells us that no man knows the day or the hour when Jesus will come again, but we can trust He "is" coming! He will come to gather those who have chosen Him as Savior and judge those who have not. Do not wait! If you have not asked Jesus to come into your life, forgive you of your sins, and be your Savior, there is no better time than right now. Today is the perfect time.

ON TIME DELIVERY

DELIVERY ON TIME, DEVOTION 5
Max Sinclair // *Children's Director*

For most of my adult life, I think the most joy that I have ever had is realizing that what I ordered from Amazon is on my front porch. It is like a mini Christmas morning for adults who already know what was ordered. This small, yet major sense of joy is just awesome, from books to movies and bobbleheads of past Presidents that arrive by mail; just waiting for me to rip into and order more. This sense of overwhelming satisfaction is further intensified by it being delivered on time. Because I am a nerd and a dork most of the time, I imagine how it arrived; was it by rail, or plane, or just on a truck? The possibilities are endless. As awesome as that being what it is, we need to look at something far more important and precious of a delivery that helped the world.

The death of Christ and His fulfillment of the scriptures of the Old Testament were necessary and right on time. We see this in the prophet Isaiah's writing in chapter 54, **"For a brief moment I deserted you, but with great compassion I will gather you"** (verse 7). This verse does not necessarily explain the Lord's timing, but it does, however, show His will and its perfect manifestation. You see God is just, and being that as it is, God must demand the payment that comes with sin, by which is death. With that being the punishment for our sin, a delivery of grace and mercy was sent, His Son and the second part of the Holy Trinity, Jesus Christ. As Christ waited to be sent, God showed His divine providence to the children of Israel to prepare the way for His Son, the Messiah. So as the people of Israel stumbled and failed, God had told Isaiah, **"In overflowing anger for a moment I hid my face from you…"** (verse 8). God had left the temple and the children of Israel; for around 400 years the God of the patriarchs of faith had been silent to His chosen people. Verse 8 continues, **"But with everlasting love I will have compassion on you, says the Lord, your Redeemer."** Based on that everlasting love and compassion, the Creator of the Universe sent His Son to show us the way and poured His wrath and the punishment for our sin on Him so that we may have a relationship with Him.

DELIVERY ON TIME DEVOTION 5

Throughout our lives, we will lose touch and forget that everything in life is in His timing. Even our salvation and the promises of God and the blessings that come with it are in His timing. We need to remember even in this season of rejoicing for the debt that was paid and His resurrection, that these things come in His time.

NO LEDGE

DELIVERY ON TIME, DEVOTION 6
John Hubbard // *Worship Leader*

I have always loved movies with an opening scene that has some huge and intricate accident. I picture a man sitting outside a restaurant doing a crossword in the newspaper when he accidentally hits his coffee cup causing the waitress to jump out of the way which startles the bicyclist who swerves to miss her. The biker ends up on the street, so the car coming behind him slams on his brakes and gets rear-ended. I have always liked the idea these types of scenes can show that sometimes the smallest of accidents can cause real problems. How could the man have known that spilling his coffee would ruin the rear bumper of a car in the street? He could not have; one of the crazy things about God is that nothing surprises Him. His plan and will do not get redirected; He does not get sent on detours, everything comes together just how He intended.

In the book of Acts, Peter is addressing multitudes of people immediately after the disciples have been speaking to them in many different languages, He talks about the coming of the Messiah, and he says an interesting thing about Jesus.

"This Jesus, delivered up according to the definite plan and foreknowledge of God, you crucified and killed by the hands of lawless men." Acts 2:23

God's definite plan of redemption for all of us was incredibly timed. Jesus was born of the line of King David, out of Bethlehem which was David's hometown. God did not have a "rough idea" of how it would play out. He knew that the Jewish leadership would reject Jesus, and they despised Him enough to plot to have Him killed. Since Jesus lived in a time of Roman occupation, who better to execute Jesus than the Romans. Even though they acted of their reasoning, God was in control of it. Jesus fully intended to die for the sins of all of us, even if it looked like a betrayal by His own people at the time.

DELIVERY ON TIME DEVOTION 6

When Peter spoke to all these people about the prophecies of Jesus being fulfilled, the Bible says that three thousand souls were saved that day.

DELIVERY ON TIME DEVOTION 6

02
DELIVERY STATUS

DR. RANDY T. JOHNSON,
GROWTH PASTOR

DELIVERY STATUS WEEK 2

I am a fan of Amazon Prime. Our family uses it for everyday essentials to unique gifts. We have purchased flowers, books, clothing, food, furniture, and workout equipment. Someday, we may buy a car or house online. My wife and I like to surprise our parents and children from time to time with random gifts. Part of the thrill is that in most cases the order gets there in two days. I cannot wait for them to get the surprise package.

What is the funniest thing you have purchased online?
_____
_____
_____

I am not a fan of checking the delivery status on normal orders. Part of the problem is I check it too often. I hate waiting for an order to "leave the station." I do not want to read, "Undeliverable" or "Attempted delivery." There is no way I would have missed the delivery. Even worse, is finding out the item's "point of origin" is China.

Knowing where something is delivered from helps us plan better for the future. Likewise, it is important to know from where or what we have been delivered.

One of the most intriguing stories in the Bible occurs in Genesis 32. Jacob wrestles with God. As the morning approaches and the match begins to end, Jacob realizes who it was and asks for a blessing. Genesis 32:30 reports his response, **"So Jacob called the name of the place Peniel, saying, 'For I have seen God face to face, and yet my life has been delivered.'"**

DELIVERY STATUS WEEK 2

What does the word *"delivered"* mean and imply?
_____
_____
_____

From what was Jacob *"delivered?"*
_____
_____
_____

How was he and how are we *"delivered?"*
_____
_____
_____

Scripture points out that there are at least four things we are delivered from when we become followers of Jesus Christ.

1. Christians are delivered from *"the domain of darkness."*

Colossians 1:13 states this point very directly, *"He has delivered us from the domain of darkness and transferred us to the kingdom of his beloved Son."* Acts 26:18 adds, *"To open their eyes, so that they may turn from darkness to light and from the power of Satan to God, that they may receive forgiveness of sins and a place among those who are sanctified by faith in me."* The concept of light and darkness is so prevalent in Scripture, that 2 Corinthians 11:14 says, *"And no wonder, for even Satan disguises himself as an angel of light."*

From what are Christians delivered?
_____
_____
_____

DELIVERY STATUS WEEK 2

To what are Christians delivered?

_____
_____
_____

2. Christians are often delivered from **"deadly peril."**

As Christians, we know God is watching out for us. Paul speaks of dangerous events in 2 Corinthians 1:10, **"He delivered us from such a deadly peril, and he will deliver us. On him we have set our hope that he will deliver us again."** We also see this kind of deliverance in Luke 8:23, **"And as they sailed he fell asleep. And a windstorm came down on the lake, and they were filling with water and were in danger."** The word **"danger"** has also been translated *"jeopardy, great danger, close to sinking, and deadly peril."*

When was a time in your life that God "saved" you physically?

_____
_____
_____

3. Christians are delivered from **"the wrath of God."**

To better understand a word, it is helpful sometimes to see synonyms for the word. However, there are times when it is better to understand the antonym. To get a better understanding of what **"wrath"** is, it is necessary to look at its antonym, **"peace."**

Romans 5:1 speaks of having peace with God, **"Therefore, since we have been justified by faith, we have peace with God through our Lord Jesus Christ."** It is a blessing to be at peace with another, especially God. The Bible takes it a step further in Philippians 4:7, **"And the peace of God, which surpasses all understanding, will**

DELIVERY STATUS WEEK 2

guard your hearts and your minds in Christ Jesus." Not only do Christians have *"peace with God"* they receive the *"peace of God."*

What is the difference between *"peace with God"* and *"peace of God?"*

_____
_____
_____

The Bible speaks of two eternal destinies. We refer to them as Heaven and Hell. John 3:36 describes them as eternal life and the other as not too promising, *"Whoever believes in the Son has eternal life; whoever does not obey the Son shall not see life, but the wrath of God remains on him."* Christians are delivered from a place where you do not see life – death. They are also delivered from the wrath of God. God was and is so creative in creation; I do not want to imagine how creative He could be in destruction.

Romans 5:9 adds to this thought of being delivered from the wrath of God, *"Since, therefore, we have now been justified by his blood, much more shall we be saved by him from the wrath of God."*

How do you picture the *"wrath of God?"*

_____
_____
_____

4. Christians are delivered from Hell and perishing.

Christians are delivered from a place of perishing (Hell) to the place of eternal life (Heaven). That is why John 3:16 is so often displayed and quoted, *"For God so loved the world, that he gave his only*

DELIVERY STATUS WEEK 2

Son, that whoever believes in him should not perish but have eternal life." John later repeats this concept, *"I give them eternal life, and they will never perish, and no one will snatch them out of my hand"* (10:28).

What image or memory comes to mind when you read, *"no one will snatch them out of my hand?"*

_____
_____
_____

In 1 Corinthians 1:18, we read, *"For the word of the cross is folly to those who are perishing, but to us who are being saved it is the power of God."*

What does that mean?

_____
_____
_____

A final thought, 2 Peter 2:6-8 describes God delivering a few before He destroyed the wicked cities, *"If by turning the cities of Sodom and Gomorrah to ashes he condemned them to extinction, making them an example of what is going to happen to the ungodly; and if he rescued righteous Lot, greatly distressed by the sensual conduct of the wicked (for as that righteous man lived among them day after day, he was tormenting his righteous soul over their lawless deeds that he saw and heard)."*

DELIVERY STATUS WEEK 2

From memory, describe Lot. Does this passage surprise you on how he is described?

_____
_____
_____

How does this story picture us and the future deliverance?

_____
_____
_____

"Saving us is the greatest and most concrete demonstration of God's love, the definitive display of His grace throughout time and eternity." - David Jeremiah

"You will find all true theology summed up in these two short sentences: Salvation is all of the grace of God. Damnation is all of the will of man." - Charles Spurgeon

DELIVERY STATUS WEEK 2

DELIVERY STATUS WEEK 2

SIN

DELIVERY STATUS, DEVOTION 1
Katrina Young // Nursery & Pre-K Director

"*He has delivered us from the domain of darkness and transferred us to the kingdom of his beloved Son, in whom we have redemption, the forgiveness of sins*" (Colossians 1:13-14).

In my B.C. days (before Christ), there were many areas of my life that I thought I would never overcome. I was, without a doubt, a slave to the darkness and incapable of victory. I will admit, some of those areas that seemed to control me still have influence and try to come roaring back. Battling fear, anxiety, and even depression would be impossible without my Savior.

The verse that I can hold onto is 2 Corinthians 5:17, **"Therefore, if anyone is in Christ, he is a new creation. The old has passed away; behold, the new has come."** Being born again is about being rescued from the old ways and choosing to live a life that God intended, walking away from the life that once enslaved me, and embracing the freedom His death and resurrection gave me.

So why do we continue to struggle after surrendering our lives to Him? The enemy is so good at reminding us of where we were and wanting us to stay in that mindset of guilt and condemnation.

Romans 8:1-2 tells us, **"There is therefore now no condemnation for those who are in Christ Jesus. For the law of the Spirit of life has set you free in Christ Jesus from the law of sin and death."**

Romans 6:4 tells us that since we have been buried and resurrected with Christ, we are now able to walk in that newness of life, unlike the unbeliever who is still a slave to sin. We can do this because Jesus has set us free from the slavery of sin and we are no longer under its penalty of death and separation from God.

DELIVERY STATUS DEVOTION 1

John 8:36 adds, *"So if the Son sets you free, you will be free indeed."*

SATAN'S FAMILY

DELIVERY STATUS, DEVOTION 2

Tommy Youngquist // *Children's Pastor*

Imagine with me that you are on a flight to Japan. While crossing the Pacific, your plane goes down and lands on a secluded island. You survived, but you do not remember who you are, where you live, or what your purpose is. Worse yet, this island has no light. It is completely dark. After being stuck on this island for sixty days, you see a faint light in the distance. Then you hear the sound of the helicopter getting louder as the light grows bigger. It is a rescue team! Someone is there to save you from this dominion of darkness, loneliness, and ultimately a slow death. How would you react to this helicopter pilot?

In Colossians 1:12-14, the Bible says: **"Giving thanks to the Father, who has qualified you to share in the inheritance of the saints in light. He has delivered us from the domain of darkness and transferred us to the kingdom of his beloved Son, in whom we have redemption, the forgiveness of sins."**

Paul was telling us that if we believe in Jesus, we are rescued from something far greater than our earlier scenario. We are rescued from the domain of darkness here on earth and for eternity. Not only are we rescued, but we are transferred to an even better situation than we could have ever imagined. We are transferred into the kingdom of Jesus!

When you start to understand the gravity of the situation in which you dwelled and from what Jesus saved you, a deep love starts to form for your Savior. Satan enslaved you to the point of death, but Jesus saved you from him. It is incredible to think about that salvation! Then, once you get it, your love for that Savior and His grace towards you turns into motivation to live for Him. You start acting in a manner worthy of the family to which you have been adopted. You can look forward to your inheritance in Heaven. Most of all, you are excited about the prospect of spending eternity with the One who has done all of this for you.

DELIVERY STATUS DEVOTION 2

Realize something church family, on our own we live in a world with no purpose, nowhere to go, and nothing to look forward. But when you *"Confess with your mouth that Jesus is Lord and believe with your heart that God raised Him from the dead"* (Romans 10:9-10), you are saved from that domain of darkness and transferred to the kingdom of Jesus. This is an incredible thing to celebrate today!

HELL

DELIVERY STATUS, DEVOTION 3

Donna Fox // *Assistant to the Growth Pastor*

If I asked you if you want to spend eternity in Heaven, or in Hell, you would say Heaven I bet. I have never met anyone who honestly said they want to spend eternity in Hell. But why, then, do we live in sin, live following Satan rather than following Jesus as Lord and Savior? We are all born into sin. Romans 3:23 says, **"For everyone has sinned; we all fall short of God's glorious standard."** We need to realize that we are sinners and we need Jesus for salvation. How do we receive this free gift? Is it by anything we do or say? Is it a one-time prayer said at VBS as a child that was not understood and changed nothing? Is it by good works? No, none of these. It is by Jesus and Jesus alone!

"He has delivered us from the domain of darkness and transferred us to the kingdom of his beloved Son."
Colossians 1:13

The 'He' referred to here is God. His beloved son is Jesus! He lifts us up from the depths of Hell and transfers us to His Kingdom – Heaven! What a glorious day when a sinner confesses he or she is a sinner, repents, and makes Jesus the Lord and Savior over their life, living for God's glory and the promise of Heaven.

Through Jesus, we are delivered from the darkness into the light. It is from Hell into Heaven. God created the light (Genesis 1:3). God created everything, including Hell. It is not His desire for us to spend eternity there, but we have a choice to make.

What does it mean to be delivered? The first thing that comes to my mind is a newborn baby being delivered. A baby is in the womb, in darkness. Then labor starts and they are delivered into the light. Fast forward to a believer's confession; some call this being "reborn." It is the same concept, leaving the darkness, entering the light. Both of these birth's come from God. He is the only one that can deliver us from our sin into His glorious kingdom.

DELIVERY STATUS DEVOTION 3

We do not deserve it. We did not do anything to earn it. We did nothing; God just transferred us to His kingdom because of our trust in Him as Lord and Savior at the time of salvation. If we are saved, He has delivered us from Hell.

We must believe in the death, burial, and resurrection of Jesus to be saved and then we are assured of this deliverance from Hell.

Jesus came and made a way for us to be delivered, to be rescued, to be set free from Satan's power. Because God sent Jesus, and Jesus died on the cross, today we have the hope of eternity in Heaven.

Have you met the God that delivers? Has he delivered you?

"All you need to do to go to Hell is do nothing." - John MacArthur

WRATH OF GOD

DELIVERY STATUS, DEVOTION 4
Brett Eberle // *Production Director*

What does it mean to be delivered from the wrath of God? I think to have an answer to that question we first have to understand what the wrath of God is. How do you understand something that you have never experienced? If you have read some of the devotions that I have previously written, then you know that I played football at Clarkston High School. One of the most important aspects of a football team is their playbook. If the opposing team were to get a hold of your playbook, they would know every move that you have ever made or will ever make in a game. That means you do not have to play the other team to experience and understand what they are going to do. The best part about God is that He handed us His playbook. The Bible is filled with examples of God's wrath, and the reasons that it was poured out.

Romans 2:5 says that the wicked store up wrath for the day of God's righteous judgment and it is because our hearts were hard. We should fear the wrath of God. Jeremiah 30:23 describes that wrath of God as a storm hurling down on the wicked. I do not know about you, but that scares me in ways that I cannot even describe. I have made mistakes, and I continue to make mistakes, and there are days that I flat out feel like I am a wicked person. Knowing that the wrath of God is hurled down terrifies me.

Just like any playbook you have to read the whole thing to understand the full game plan and the Bible is no different; if you stop halfway through you only see half of the plan. You have to finish the book to understand the most important part, that God's wrath is satisfied with Christ.

Romans 3:26 says, **"It was to show his righteousness at the present time, so that he might be just and the justifier of the one who has faith in Jesus."**

DELIVERY STATUS DEVOTION 4

What Jesus did for us is the game plan to which the whole playbook points. Because of what Jesus did, God's wrath will not come hurling down on my wickedness and myself. Just because I know His wrath will not come hurling down, that does not mean that I do not respect and fear the power that God has. As important as it is that we fear God, it is just as important that our fear points us to gratitude for what Jesus did for us. We have been delivered from the wrath of God through Jesus. Celebrate what Jesus has done for us and never forget from what He has delivered us.

SELF

DELIVERY STATUS, DEVOTION 5
Jen Combs // Wife of Lead Pastor Joshua Combs

Romans 7:18-21 says, *"For I know that nothing good dwells in me, that is, in my flesh. For I have the desire to do what is right, but not the ability to carry it out. For I do not do the good I want, but the evil I do not want is what I keep on doing. Now if I do what I do not want, it is no longer I who do it, but sin that dwells within me. So I find it to be a law that when I want to do right, evil lies close at hand."*

Paul is telling us how he is constantly battling self. Every day he goes to battle crucifying the flesh of the evil it wants. Our fleshly desires are in opposition to godly desires. What are some examples of things the flesh desires?

Galatians 5:19-21 says, *"Now the works of the flesh are evident: sexual immorality, impurity, sensuality, idolatry, sorcery, enmity, strife, jealousy, fits of anger, rivalries, dissensions, divisions, envy, drunkenness, orgies."*

Ever struggle with any of these? Ugh, that in and of itself is just depressing. You are probably thinking, "Awesome, so I just have to battle these things every day, all day, and it never goes away."

Colossians 1:13-14 adds, *"He has delivered us from the domain of darkness and transferred us to the kingdom of His beloved Son, in whom we have redemption, the forgiveness of sins."*

I had the opportunity to visit one of the ladies prisons a few days ago. I met a woman named Tabitha. I asked her if she knew Jesus as her Savior. She told me, yes, but she did not understand how God could forgive her if she could not forgive herself. This is where the battle of self began. Tabitha was battling the shame and guilt that she had for whatever she had done. I was able to assure her that when she gave Jesus her life, He took her shame and guilt and in return offered forgiveness. It was no longer hers to bare.

DELIVERY STATUS DEVOTION 5

Satan wants to keep throwing temptations at you. Sometimes they are mind games that you are worthless, not good enough, guilt and shame. Other times it is outward temptations to lust, get drunk, or to pop those pills.

1 Corinthians 10:13 tells us, **"...God is faithful, and he will not let you be tempted beyond your ability, but with the temptation he will also provide the way of escape, that you may be able to endure it."**

If you know Jesus as your Savior, you have truly given your life to Him; Scripture says that you have been delivered. What does delivered mean? Webster's defines it as "set free." You have been set free from battling the flesh alone. The Lord is committed to helping you battle. If you do not know Him, you are left to battle alone. Let me tell you, that is not pretty. I have watched countless people think that they can fight anger, bitterness, and the list of addictions all on their own. Maybe today you find yourself alone, tired, angry, and sad because things just are not working. They are not working because you are battling alone.

Come to Jesus and let Him join in your fight.

CHAINS

DELIVERY STATUS, DEVOTION 6
Isaiah Combs // *Worship Leader & Young Adults Director*

My favorite Christmas movie is The Muppet Christmas Carol. It is the Charles Dickens Classic tale remade with the goofiness of the Muppets. I am a sucker for any Muppets' movies. I may or may not force my children to watch them with me. We may or may not sing all the songs along with the Muppets, but that is another story.

There is a scene in The Muppet Christmas Carol that I want to point out. So, if you know anything about the story, Ebenezer Scrooge has two partners that pass away. They are brothers named Jacob and Robert Marley. In the Muppets version, the Marley Brothers are played by Satler and Waldorf. They are two grumpy old men who heckle everyone. In the movie, the Marley brothers come to warn Scrooge about the evil things he is doing and the afterlife effects of the things he does. The two brothers are covered in chains that drag and hold them down. They tell Scrooge that they had built the chain links from all the mean and nasty deeds they had done throughout there lives. Then they warn Scrooge about how many chains that he has built up and has coming for him in his afterlife. Of course, they do this through song and dance.

It reminds me about the chains we have. We were chained to death. Romans 6:23 says, **"For the wages of sin is death."**

Just like in the Muppets movie, we build chains and are chained to death like a prisoner. I like to replace the word **"wages"** with the word "cost." The cost of our sin is death. The chains are the cost for lives of sin.

The verse continues, **"BUT"** (I am so thankful for the "buts" in the Bible).

"But the free gift of God is eternal life in Christ Jesus our Lord."

DELIVERY STATUS DEVOTION 6

There is freedom from the chains that we have made in life. It is a free gift that comes only through Jesus (our chain breaker).

Colossians 1:13-14 adds, *"He has delivered us from the domain of darkness and transferred us to the kingdom of his beloved Son, in whom we have redemption, the forgiveness of sins."*

There is freedom from the domain of darkness (our prison in chains), and through the Son (Jesus) there is redemption and forgiveness(freedom).

I am thankful that I have been set free from chains of sin (I am also thankful I am not Ebenezer Scrooge and had three ghosts visit me).

DELIVERY STATUS DEVOTION 6

03

DELIVERY MAN

CALEB COMBS,
GATHERING PASTOR

DELIVERY MAN WEEK 3

"**T**hen the Lord said, 'I have surely seen the affliction of my people who are in Egypt and have heard their cry because of their taskmasters. I know their sufferings, and I have come down to deliver them...'" (Exodus 3:7-8a).

When I think of the delivery man, I think of one thing in particular... pizza! I love pizza. I could eat pizza for breakfast, lunch, and dinner, and then warm up the leftovers for a midnight snack. I am particular about my pizza and just want meat on it, no veggies! Ahh, a nice warm "meatza" with flavored crust; there is nothing better in the world (okay- a bit of an exaggeration, but you get where I am going with this).

What is one of the best things about that fresh, hot, tasty (now I am starting to get hungry) pizza? You can have one delivered. I do not have to leave my house or miss any of the big game, and a guy knocks on my door delivering a slice of Heaven. Now this man did not make the pizza, and he most likely did not even take the order. He simply was used (or in most cases paid) to deliver a gift. Okay, maybe it is a "cheesy" analogy (okay, really now I am done), but throughout the Bible, we see many examples of God using men and women to deliver His people. From Noah to the Apostle Paul, we have many examples to study. One of the most famous deliverers used by God in the Bible is Moses. Christians and non-Christians alike know the famous story of God sending the plagues and parting the water, which ultimately led to the children of Israel being freed from the hand of Pharaoh and the Egyptians. There is a lot more to that story. Grab your Bibles and let us check it out.

How did the Israelites end up in Egypt? (see Genesis 47)

_____
_____
_____

DELIVERY MAN WEEK 3

Why were the Egyptians afraid of the Israelites?
_____
_____
_____

God's children were crying out to Him in Exodus 2:24. Why were they?
_____
_____
_____

God's children, the Israelites, were slaves to the Egyptians, and they were subject to cruel and extreme measures to keep them captive and to control their population. Exodus 1:13-14 tells us, *"So they ruthlessly made the people of Israel work as slaves and made their lives bitter with hard service, in mortar and brick, and in all kinds of work in the field. In all their work they ruthlessly made them work as slaves."* They were beaten, dehumanized, and even killed to make sure they were kept in their place.

Exodus 2:23 adds, *"During those many days the king of Egypt died, and the people of Israel groaned because of their slavery and cried out for help. Their cry for rescue from slavery came up to God."*

God's children were enslaved by the Egyptians, and they cried out for rescue, and God heard them and came to their rescue. He knew that on their own they would not be able to escape, and so He recruited a "delivery man" to help them.

Psalm 34:17 (NLT) says, *"The LORD hears his people when they call to him for help. He rescues them from all their troubles."*

DELIVERY MAN WEEK 3

What do you know about the life of Moses? (Hint: Check out the Book of Exodus)

_____
_____
_____

How did God get Moses' attention?

_____
_____
_____

Exodus 3:10 says, **"Come, I will send you to Pharaoh that you may bring my people, the children of Israel, out of Egypt."**

Where and what was Moses doing when he was called by God? Why was he there?

_____
_____
_____

Have you ever felt God calling you to do something? Explain.

_____
_____
_____

"God is calling you, equipping you, and preparing you according to His purpose." Unknown

God has called us all to something. Whether that is sharing the Gospel with a family member, neighbor, coworker, or a friend, we are all given a mission to reach the world with the Good News of Jesus. However, I can think of many instances where I felt God lead me to do something and I fought with Him or made an excuse on

DELIVERY MAN WEEK 3

why I should not do it. From giving money to something or someone to calling someone to apologize or work through an issue, God leads and directs us, and we need to respond to His calling.

How did Moses respond to God's call in his life?
(Read Exodus 3:11-22)

_____
_____
_____

What excuses have you made to God?

_____
_____
_____

Exodus 3:11 adds, *"But Moses said to God, 'Who am I that I should go to Pharaoh and bring the children of Israel out of Egypt?'"*

God used Moses to deliver His people from the hand of the Egyptians. He was used to do many miracles and to lead the people, but it was not easy. Moses was human after all and had many imperfections, character flaws, and he certainly made mistakes. Despite this, God continued to use him. God promised to deliver His people, and He did just that. He got the attention of Pharaoh and the Egyptians with several plagues, and on the tenth one, Pharaoh folded and released the Israelites from captivity. In Exodus chapter 12, we see the last plague unfold leading to Pharaoh telling Moses to take his people and go. This was not the end of the story as we know from reading the Old Testament because God had to use many other people to deliver His people. From Kings to Judges to Prophets, one thing we know is that God is faithful and He will deliver His people if they cry out to Him.

Isaiah 6:8 says, *"And I heard the voice of the Lord saying, 'Whom shall I send, and who will go for us?' Then I said, 'Here I am! Send me.'"*

I love the words that Isaiah speaks, *"Here I am, Send Me!"* These words are more than words; they are a mindset, God use me! There is a problem in this world, and it is called sin. Millions of people are enslaved to it. Just as the Egyptians were to the Israelites, sin is ruthless and will bind us in chains and eventually kill us. But God sent a Man to deliver us, and it was His Son. Jesus Christ died on the cross to deliver us from death and lead us into freedom, freedom from sin and freedom from death. What a message! Just like God called Moses to be His delivery man, we are also called to service. We have an incredible message that we can bring to the lost, in hopes that they will also be delivered from their sin. 2 Timothy chapter 2 tells us that we can be used as a vessel to reach the world. Will you accept that calling? Just like the pizza delivery guy, we need to deliver the precious gift of the Gospel on time, because we do not know how long we have to be used.

Romans 12:1 says, *"I appeal to you therefore, brothers, by the mercies of God, to present your bodies as a living sacrifice, holy and acceptable to God, which is your spiritual worship."*

How can God use you today?
___
___
___

Where is God sending you?
___
___
___

DELIVERY MAN WEEK 3

JOSEPH

DELIVERY MAN, DEVOTION 1

Sierra Combs // *Women's Ministry Director*

I love a good story, and one of my very favorites in the Bible is the story of Joseph. If you grew up in the church, you have most likely heard of him. He was the young boy with the colorful coat. It was given to him by his father Jacob, or Israel because God changed his name. This did not sit well with his brothers (he had 11 of them) because they saw the intense love that their father had for Joseph and were extremely jealous of him. They were so jealous that they threw him into a pit and sold him as a slave to some guys heading for Egypt. This is a riveting story! I encourage you to read it this week for yourself in Genesis chapters 37-50. Joseph finds himself as a slave in Egypt, but because of his gifts, wisdom, and God's blessing, he works his way up in society. This certainly was not by accident; God had this plan for Joseph the whole time. At one point, God's plan had Joseph living in comfort and success, like when he found himself in charge of a very prominent household in Egypt. Just when things started getting good, God's plan landed Joseph in prison for two years for a crime he did not commit. However, God was always working in and through Joseph's life, and regardless of his circumstances, Joseph remained a godly man of great integrity. God blessed him and used his hardships for a purpose, which eventually led to him becoming the second most important man in all of Egypt, second to Pharaoh himself.

Joseph had always been a dreamer and an interpreter of dreams. It is one of the reasons his brothers hated him so much. It is also how he got connected to Pharaoh. Because of this God-given gift, Joseph was able to warn Pharaoh of an upcoming famine that would affect all of Egypt and beyond. Joseph knew he had some time and made provisions over all the land to store food in the time of abundance. When the famine eventually came, because of Joseph's quick thinking and good managing skills, there was enough food for not just all of Egypt, but the surrounding lands as well. It becomes interesting who was included in those surrounding areas, but the very brothers that sent him to Egypt in the first place.

DELIVERY MAN DEVOTION 1

I can only imagine how Joseph must have felt. The last time he saw them was when he was looking up from a pit or looking back at them as he was taken off as a slave. They hated him and never wanted to see him again. All these years later, they meet again, with Joseph having complete control over their lives and their futures. Most would have had the brothers killed on the spot, or at least turned them away. Instead, Joseph showed them mercy and grace, **"So Joseph said to his brothers, 'Come near to me, please...I am your brother, Joseph, whom you sold into Egypt. And now do not be distressed or angry with yourselves because you sold me here, for ... God sent me before you to preserve for you a remnant on earth, and to keep alive for you many survivors"** (Genesis 45:4-7). Chapter 50 verses 20-21 (NIV) continue the story of forgiveness, **"You intended to harm me, but God intended it for good to accomplish what is now being done, the saving of many lives. So then, don't be afraid. I will provide for you and your children."** Not only did Joseph provide food for his brothers, but he also moved the entire family to Egypt and provided them with the best land in all the region. While Joseph's brothers were afraid he would seek revenge for what they had done, Joseph recognized God's sovereign plan to use him to deliver His people, the young nation of Israel.

It is good to do a little recap on Joseph. He was a shepherd to his father's sheep. He was loved deeply by his father, and despised by his brothers and others who wanted to harm him. He was sold for the price of a slave. He was tempted, falsely accused, and bound in chains. Life was difficult, and he suffered greatly, but he overcame and was exalted to the second highest position, seated at the right hand of the king. He forgave those who wronged him and delivered his people from death. Does it sound familiar? Perhaps one of the biggest reasons I love the story of Joseph is because it is a beautiful foreshadowing of another that would come. While Joseph was a deliverer, Jesus is "the" Deliverer. He was also a shepherd to His Father's sheep. He was loved deeply by the Father, and despised by His people. He was sold for the price of a slave, tempted, falsely accused, and bound in chains. His life was difficult, and He suffered greatly. However, He overcame and was exalted to the highest place, seated at the right hand of the Father. If we accept Him as our Savior, He forgives us and delivers us from eternal death and separation from Him. That is quite a delivery! Thank you, Jesus, for Your grace and mercy!

DELIVERY MAN DEVOTION 1

MOSES

DELIVERY MAN, DEVOTION 2
Ryan Story // *Student Pastor*

Name meanings fascinate me. When it came to naming my two sons, I had to make sure that their names had some substance behind them. Broly Ezra is my strong and valiant helper, and Ezekiel Gambit is my reminder that God strengthens with sacrifice. In almost every case in the Bible, a person's name is a gateway into their personality. To prepare for Summer Camp this year, God placed on my heart to preach on Exodus, moreover about Pharaoh and the plagues. After studying Exodus, I read somewhere that Moses name means to "draw out" or "drawn out."

Throughout the Bible, there are people or objects that are meant to be types of Christ. These types are meant to symbolize actions that Jesus would do. If you study any given story, you can see how God's plan was being displayed thousands of years before Jesus entered the scene. Moses is a type of Christ that shows how Jesus would deliver us from the world. Moses was the man God used to lead the nation of Israel out of the bondage of Egypt to the Promised Land. While in Egypt, the king (Pharaoh) refused to listen to God or Moses. In similar means, the prince of this world refuses to let us leave. Because of God's plan for Moses, he was able to be used to draw his people (also could be His people) away from the world and into a place of promise.

It is an amazing thought to realize that Jesus has drawn you out of the corrupt, sinful world in which you live. He has taken you from being a slave to being free. It should be a humble feeling knowing that because of Jesus' sacrifice, we who were once enslaved to a life of captivity are set free. 1 Peter 2:9 says what we are now, ***"But you are a chosen race, a royal priesthood, a holy nation, a people for his own possession, that you may proclaim the excellencies of him who called you out of darkness into his marvelous light."*** Because Jesus came to deliver us from the world, we have hope.

DELIVERY MAN DEVOTION 2

From what have you been drawn out? There are people in our church who have been drawn out of a world of drugs and alcohol to living truly free from bondage. There are people in our church who have been drawn out of families where abuse and violence reigned, and now they have true peace in their homes. There are people who have been drawn out of wandering and aimlessness to being used by God for His purpose. How has Jesus drawn you out of the world? How can you go about celebrating that deliverance this Easter season?

JOSHUA

DELIVERY MAN, DEVOTION 3
James Mann // *Children's Director*

Joshua is an important person in the Old Testament. He first took over the lead of the Israelites after the death of Moses. Then, he led the Israelites through the Jordan and into The Promised Land. Finally, he led the people into conquering the Canaanites and split up the country to all the different tribes. Joshua's name means "savior" and "deliverer." This is fitting because Joshua helped deliver the Israelites out of their wandering in the wilderness and into The Promised Land. This is a big deal because for the past forty years these people had been out in the desert. The people were getting unruly and impatient over this time, and the people began to question God repeatedly. If God did not use Joshua to do this, there is no telling what would have happened. One thing that is for sure is that more sin would have followed.

Joshua's road ahead of him was not easy by any means. He had to take over the reins after the death of Moses. Joshua kept questioning whether this is something he could do. We sometimes think this as we are doing the things God has commanded us to do. We must remember what God said to Joshua, *"Have I not commanded you? Be strong and courageous. Do not be frightened, and do not be dismayed, for the Lord your God is with you wherever you go"* (Joshua 1:9). Sometimes God is trying to use us to help deliver people to Him, but we are too focused on our fears to move past that and do what is needed of us. We must remember that no matter where we go, He is always with us.

Fun Fact: Both Joshua and Jesus mean savior and deliverer. Joshua and Jesus delivered people out of one situation and into another. Jesus delivered us from our sinful way, and instead of sending us directly to Hell after death, He has delivered us into His Father's hands and given us the chance of everlasting life. Much like the Israelites, this is not something we deserve. We deserve to be left in Egypt to fend for ourselves under the rule of a lunatic. We deserve to be in the wilderness, searching for any means of survival. We

DELIVERY MAN DEVOTION 3

deserve eternal pain and suffering because we sin and are all sinners and have fallen short of the glory of God. Instead, God has taken pity on us. He has spared us from eternal damnation and suffering. He sent His Son to deliver us to Him, just like He used Joshua to deliver the Israelites closer to Him.

BOAZ

DELIVERY MAN, DEVOTION 4
Debbie Kerr // *Office Administrator*

Have you ever found yourself in a painful season of life, one that found you crying out for deliverance? I am in such a season right now. The steps God has asked me to walk, basically alone in the physical sense, is caring for my dear mother in her final stage of Alzheimer's. While I feel God's presence and direction moment by moment, and consider it an extreme honor, at the same time I find myself tempted to ask why? "Why do you not take her to Heaven and end her suffering?" "Why do I have to watch her slowly slip away?" "Why have you eliminated all other family from the situation and left me alone to deal with the daily decisions and burden?" The answer is always gently revealed to me. God is using this to make me stronger in my dependence on Him. Simultaneously, my dear mom is silently teaching me what it looks like to finish well and rejoice in all circumstances. God is not only working through me but in me as well. When I feel empty or scared, I am reminded that He daily adds to our account the grace and strength needed to both my mom and me. He is our rescuer and deliverer, redeeming what has been stolen in the natural. The blessings I have received during this season are the dearest to me.

The book of Ruth is a beautiful portrait of God's grace and provision. It is a short book of only four chapters, but it is jam packed with theology and truth that we can learn from today. The main narrative in Ruth centers around the lives of a mother-in-law, Naomi, and her daughter-in-law, Ruth. After the deaths of their husbands, they remained together to help each other. These two women were struggling to make it on their own, and they were in desperate need of a rescuer. Things had gone from bad to worse. They had to flee a famine in the land and draw on all their resources to survive. I am sure they cried out to God more than once to be rescued from their present situation. They needed a kinsman redeemer. In Leviticus chapter 25 we learn that a kinsman redeemer is a male relative who, according to various laws of the Pentateuch, had the responsibility to act on behalf of a family member who was in danger, in need, or

DELIVERY MAN DEVOTION 4

in trouble. It is one who delivers and rescues the person in need or redeems their property. Through a series of events, Ruth met a man named Boaz. Boaz was a relative of Naomi's deceased husband. Ruth and Naomi plot to gain the attention of Boaz and through God's providence and provision "their" plan worked. Ruth and Boaz end up getting married thus, redeeming his bride. The account of Boaz as a kinsman redeemer foreshadows Jesus Christ, who will redeem the church for Himself. We are His bride.

Like Ruth and Naomi, you and I are in desperate need of a kinsman redeemer. We are born into the world already bankrupt and in trouble spiritually. We cannot do enough good works or redeem our souls. Jesus became the ultimate Kinsman Redeemer when He died on the cross and shed His blood as payment for our sins. He paid a debt He did not owe because we owed a debt we could not pay.

Isaiah 54:5 says, *"For your Maker is your husband, the Lord of hosts is his name; and the Holy One of Israel is your Redeemer, the God of the whole earth he is called."*

GIDEON

DELIVERY MAN, DEVOTION 5
James Clouse // *Student Pastor*

We have a lot of false idols in this world. Every false idol does not need to be a "god" like the past so-called "gods" like Zeus or the Egyptian god, Ra. In our culture alone there are numerous false gods that we do not even recognize as gods such as electronics, money, friends, or success. Anything that we put more time and effort into than we do God and our relationship with Him is a false idol.

Charles Spurgeon once said, "Revenge, lust, ambition, pride, and self-will are too often as exalted as the gods of man's idolatry; while holiness, peace, contentment, and humility are viewed as unworthy of a serious thought."

These idols are prevalent in our society and things from which we need to be delivered. To be delivered from these gods can often be difficult and uncomfortable. Gideon was also placed in an uncomfortable position when an angel of the Lord came to him.

"That night the Lord said to him, 'Take your father's bull, and the second bull seven years old, and pull down the altar of Baal that your father has, and cut down the Asherah that is beside it and build an altar to the Lord your God on the top of the stronghold here, with stones laid in due order. Then take the second bull and offer it as a burnt offering with the wood of the Asherah that you shall cut down.' So Gideon took ten men of his servants and did as the Lord had told him. But because he was too afraid of his family and the men of the town to do it by day, he did it by night" (Judges 6:25-27).

Here is a man that came from a lowly family in a group of people always on the run. God came to him to help deliver his people from the enemy and to deliver them from Baal, a false god. Gideon was asked to rid the town of their false god and the altar that was for him, and to replace it with an altar to the one true God. Gideon was afraid but did what God asked him to do.

DELIVERY MAN DEVOTION 5

Sometimes taking a step of faith and trusting God to deliver us from our "gods" can be scary, but remember that we do not need to do it by ourselves. Jesus is the only one that can truly deliver us from the gods of society. Jesus is now that altar we need to come to so that we can worship His Father. Replace the altar in your life with Jesus, and you can also be delivered.

DAVID

DELIVERY MAN, DEVOTION 6
Richie Henson // Production Director

One of the most amazing things about the Bible is the ability it has to use the Old Testament to teach us about Jesus. Just think how spectacular it is that all of the writings that came thousands of years before Jesus ever stepped foot on the earth were pointing to Him. They were preparing the way for the one Messiah whom would deliver us all from the clutches of sin and death. To me, that is the greatest Bible attribute setting it apart from all other "holy" books. The Bible is singularly focused on helping people come to know Jesus as their Savior.

With this idea in mind, I would like us to look at David and more specifically his run in with Goliath. As we read the story of David and Goliath, it is clear that the people of Israel were being held captive by the Philistines. Each day, Goliath came out and mocked the Israelites and God and each day the Israelites cowered before him. When David arrives on the scene, full of faith, he firmly believes that God desires to deliver His people from the Philistines. So, David approaches Saul about going forth as the Israelite champion.

As Saul tried to discourage David, David recounted that God had given him the strength to deliver sheep from the mouth of a lion and in turn, God will give David the strength to deliver Israel from the Philistines. We all remember how the story went from there. David took smooth stones and slings one killing Goliath. The Israelites are delivered, and they gain the strength and power they need to run into the valley and defeated the entirety of the Philistine army.

I think it is of great importance to look at this passage in light of Jesus. The giant that is sin mocks us in the valley, declaring that we are worthless and God has no power. In our time of dire need and desperation, Jesus by His death, burial, and resurrection has slung the proverbial stone of victory, casting this giant that causes such fear to the earth in a heap of defeat. In the same way, David slew the giant to provide deliverance for God's people; Jesus has defeated the giant debt of sin and death and delivered us to life eternal.

DELIVERY MAN DEVOTION 6

So, just as the Israelites were spurred on to fight valiantly following their deliverance by David, we as followers of Jesus should be even more spurred on by the deliverance we have through Jesus to fight the good fight each day, pursuing all that is holy and right in the sight of God.

DELIVERY MAN DEVOTION 6

04
DELIVERY PLAN

JOHN CARTER,
DIRECTOR OF OPERATIONS

DELIVERY PLAN WEEK 4

When we talk about preparing for death, most of us think of the "living will" we have in place, or the life insurance policy that we took out to cover expenses after we depart. No one wants to contemplate the moment they will die, let alone plan for it! Death is a pretty unsatisfying topic for sure. If we have a choice, I think most of us would like to depart in peace, in our sleep, or with no pain. Aside from the Easter bunny, Jesus' death is a critical part of the discussion around this season. Have you ever considered that it was all planned out?

It is helpful to do a little exercise with the Bible. Psalms 22 was written roughly 1000 years before Jesus' actual death. If we compare it with the Gospel books of Matthew, Mark, Luke, and John, you will start to see some fascinating comparisons. Remember the time difference between these authors, roughly 1000 years!

Compare Psalms 22:1 with Matthew 27:46 and Mark 15:34.
What phrase do you see in all three passages?
_____
_____
_____

Compare Psalms 22:7 with Matthew 27:31,39, Mark 15:20,29, Luke 22:63, and Luke 23:36.

Do you see the similar response; how do they treat Him?
_____
_____
_____

DELIVERY PLAN WEEK 4

Compare Psalms 22:8 with Matthew 27:42-43 and Mark 15:30-32. How did the Pharisees use the similar phrase in Psalms 22 to mock Jesus?

_____
_____
_____

Compare Psalms 22:16 with Matthew 27:44, Mark 15:27, Luke 23:32, and John 19:18.

What does it mean to have evildoers encircling someone? Can you see the reference to the thieves?

_____
_____
_____

Compare Psalms 22:18 with Matthew 27:35, Mark 15:24, Luke 23:34, and John 19:23-24.

What does it mean to cast lots? How do you think one would know this would happen 1000 years prior?

_____
_____
_____

There are many other aspects of Psalms 22 that can be compared to someone dying on a cross (in particular the description is verses 14-15). The medical scientific similarities are more than coincidence; what do you think?

_____
_____
_____

DELIVERY PLAN WEEK 4

I hope you can see the awesome prophecy that exists in this single passage. There are more passages that predicted the events of Jesus' death. This would indicate that somehow there was someone that knew what would happen, right?

_____
_____
_____

Take some time and read Isaiah 53 (this was written hundreds of years before Jesus walked on earth and was crucified). How clearly do you see the similarity between the passage in Isaiah and what happened to Jesus on the cross?

_____
_____
_____

So here is the big question, do you think there was a plan or did it all happen accidentally?

_____
_____
_____

Think about these questions for a while:
Do you think it was an accident that Jesus was betrayed by Judas? Was it a coincidence that Pilate washed his hands of Jesus? Was it mere "happenstance" that the religious leaders of Israel despised Jesus? Was it a random act that the Roman soldiers beat Jesus and gambled for his clothing?

What does the lack of coincidence mean or indicate about Jesus?

_____
_____
_____

DELIVERY PLAN WEEK 4

Do you think Jesus knew what was going to happen to Him before it happened?

_____
_____
_____

Read Matthew 17:22-23. What is Jesus predicting will happen?

_____
_____
_____

Read Mark 8:31-33. Why would Jesus rebuke Peter over this saying?

_____
_____
_____

What do you think it means to set your mind on the things of God versus the things of man?

_____
_____
_____

If we think in human terms, we will never understand the truth and richness of what God planned for us.

Ephesians 2:1-5; 8-10

"And you were dead in the trespasses and sins in which you once walked, following the course of this world, following the prince of the power of the air, the spirit that is now at work in the sons of disobedience— among whom we all once lived in the passions of our flesh, carrying out the desires of the body and the mind, and were by nature children of wrath, like the rest of mankind. But God, being rich in mercy, because of the great

love with which he loved us, even when we were dead in our trespasses, made us alive together with Christ."

"For by grace you have been saved through faith. And this is not your own doing; it is the gift of God, not a result of works, so that no one may boast. For we are his workmanship, created in Christ Jesus for good works, which God prepared beforehand, that we should walk in them."

When we plan for our death, it is because we know that death is inevitable; so we plan often with the intention of benefiting those we care about most.

Do you think Jesus had to die? Did God have to give up His Son to come to earth?

_____
_____
_____

Philippians 2:5-8
"Have this mind among yourselves, which is yours in Christ Jesus, who, though he was in the form of God, did not count equality with God a thing to be grasped, but made himself nothing, taking the form of a servant, being born in the likeness of men. And being found in human form, he humbled himself by becoming obedient to the point of death, even death on a cross."

As I walk through the plan that God had for Jesus and for me, I cannot help but ask, "Why?" Why would God do that for me? Why would he give up so much, just for me? If you can understand it, He did it for you as well! Why do you think he would do that?

_____
_____
_____

DELIVERY PLAN WEEK 4

The answer, which is hard for me to fully put into words is because He sees me as something of value. He considered my life as something worth saving, so much so, that He put into motion a plan to deliver me from my destruction and sin long before I was even born. It is really hard to fully understand how God works His plan, but we can see that He did have a plan, and His plan included you and me. To finish up, contemplate how this plan of God includes you.

How was and is the "delivery plan" for you?
_____
_____
_____

Can you see that without the "delivery plan" we would not have a solution or an answer for our condition?
_____
_____
_____

Does the knowledge of knowing that God has a plan give you encouragement that there is a purpose and a plan for you?
_____
_____
_____

How will you apply the knowledge of the "delivery plan" to your life and how you worship God?
_____
_____
_____

DELIVERY PLAN WEEK 4

DELIVERY PLAN WEEK 4

JUDAS

DELIVERY PLAN, DEVOTION 1
Ryan Story // *Student Pastor*

There are two major schools of thought in the Christian theological world. If you ever want to start major arguments between biblical scholars say the words "predestination" or "free will," and then run for cover. These conversations can be fascinating in which to listen and participate. There are Bible juggernauts on both sides. Both sides use Scripture, love Jesus, want to see the lost saved and should love those with opposing views. One of the biggest points of contention with the Arminian and Calvinism crowd is found in one man, Judas Iscariot. The issue becomes, did Judas choose to betray Jesus, or was he predestined to betray our Lord? Did he have a choice at all or does God make it so people have no out and have to commit horrible acts? So the great theological question of the day is, did God use Judas for His glory?

There are some interesting Scripture verses about Judas that can help figure out if Judas was predestined to betray, or if he had to make that choice. If you read any of the Gospels, every time Judas is mentioned there is never a positive linked to it. The writers always make sure we know that Judas was the one who betrayed Jesus. John 6:70-71 says, **"Jesus answered them, 'Did I not choose you, the twelve? And yet one of you is a devil.' He spoke of Judas the son of Simon Iscariot, for he, one of the twelve, was going to betray him."** I cannot imagine a worse thing to be known for all eternity that you were a devil! Again in John 13:27, Jesus says that **"Satan entered into Judas."** Now, if we like to use verses in the Bible that say God knows the plans He has for us, sometimes that plan is not always the nicest. If you read Zechariah 11 and Jeremiah 32, many believe that Judas' betrayal was prophesied thousands of years before it happened. So, in this case, Judas' fate was set. God knew the devil would get him; God knew who and what Judas was. God has to use evil because whenever He ever uses humans, that is the only choice He has.

DELIVERY PLAN DEVOTION 1

That has always scared me that God could use me in a manner like that. God can use us like He used Pharaoh, Nebuchadnezzar, or King Saul. God's plan for us can sometimes be set in stone to be an example of what not to be. While I almost set that as a hyper predestination truth in my head, I read Matthew 27:3-5.

"Then when Judas, his betrayer, saw that Jesus was condemned, he changed his mind and brought back the thirty pieces of silver to the chief priests and the elders, saying, 'I have sinned by betraying innocent blood.' They said, 'What is that to us? See to it yourself.' And throwing down the pieces of silver into the temple, he departed, and he went and hanged himself."

After Jesus' arrest, Judas seemed to feel some sort of remorse. He understood the gravity of what he just did. However, I only see Judas showing remorse, but not repentance. Judas admits he did wrong, he admits Jesus was innocent, but he never called out for salvation. While reading this, I wonder what if Judas waited three more days before he took his life? When Jesus rose from the grave, He redeemed Peter. I am curious what Jesus would have said to Judas. Judas took away his opportunity for redemption.

God used Judas; that fact is undeniable. However, was God done with Judas? That is the ten-million-dollar question. What if He had more planned for Judas?

PILATE

DELIVERY PLAN, DEVOTION 2
Lorna Lyman

Pontius Pilate was a Roman religious official. He was appointed to his position in 26 AD. He was governor of Judea. His two main jobs were to keep order in the country and make sure all taxes were collected and sent to Rome. He held this position for about ten years. Pilate was a stubborn, cruel man and had very little respect for the Jewish people. Most of Judea hated the Romans.

An uprising could develop quickly over a small dispute. This happened quite often during Passover. Roman governors were always present during the Passover, and Pilate wanted to keep the peace. Pilate was very careful about avoiding the Jewish religious leaders unless they threatened him personally.

The Jewish leaders delivered Jesus to Pilate's residence hoping that Pilate would grant his execution. John 18:29-30 says, **"So Pilate went outside to them and said, 'What accusation do you bring against this man?' They answered him, 'If this man were not doing evil, we would not have delivered him over to you.'"** Under the Roman law they did not have enough evidence that Jesus is guilty of any capital offense; therefore, they are having a hard time convincing Pilate that Jesus should be put to death.

The story continues in John chapter 18:33-38. Pilate and Jesus had a conversation. Pilate started to question Jesus if He was the King of the Jews. Jesus explained to him that He is a King, but His kingdom is not of this world. If He were of this world, His servants would fight to save Him. Pilate asked, **"So you are a King?"** Jesus answered, **"You say that I am a king"** and went on to tell Pilate that His purpose of coming to earth was to bear witness to the truth. Pilate then questioned Jesus, **"What is truth?"** Pilate fails to see that he is standing face to face with the One who said, **"I am the truth."** Pilate is spiritually blind to the truth that is right in front of him. Pilate is about to deliver Jesus to His death.

DELIVERY PLAN DEVOTION 2

Pilate lacked interest in Jesus' case and just wanted it to go away. Unfortunately, he is up against an angry mob. It was the custom at the Feast of the Passover for Pilate to release a prisoner. Since he did not think Jesus was guilty, he decided to give the people two choices: Jesus, the king of the Jews or Barabbas a robber and a murderer. The Jewish chief priests and elders had gathered enough people to be on their side to ask for Barabbas to be freed and for Jesus to be killed. The angry crowd shouted for Jesus to be crucified and for Barabbas to be freed.

Pilate then has a second conversation with Jesus (John 19:9-11). He asks Jesus, *"Where are you from?"* Jesus does not answer. Pilate asks, *"Do you not know that I have authority to release you and authority to crucify you?"* Jesus answered, *"You would have no authority over me at all unless it had been given you from above. Therefore he who delivered me over to you has the greater sin."* Once again Pilate remained convinced that Jesus was not guilty. He continued to try and release Jesus. The Jews and religious leaders continued to oppose Pilate and shout, *"Crucify him."* There was an uprising starting, and if he did not handle it properly, it would harm his political career. Finally, Pilate feeling like he had no other choice, gave into their demand and released Barabbas. He took water and washed his hands in front of the crowd (Matthew 27:24). This was a symbolic gesture in that he did not believe Jesus deserved death and did not approve of His crucifixion. However, this does not release him from his guilt for taking part in the death of Jesus. He delivered Jesus over to the Jews to be put to death, and he aided in their plans by having Roman soldiers conduct the crucifixion. Pilate delivered Jesus to His death knowing that Jesus was innocent.

Without Pilate sentencing Jesus to death, Jesus would not have fulfilled Scripture that he had to die on the cross for our sins. It was to restore the fullness of the righteousness of God that was planned for us. God ordained Jesus to go to Calvary.

RELIGIOUS LEADERS

DELIVERY PLAN, DEVOTION 3
Mark O'Connor // *Student Director*

After Jesus raised Lazarus from the dead, John 11:48-50 says, *"'If we let him go on like this, everyone will believe in him, and the Romans will come and take away both our place and our nation.' But one of them, Caiaphas, who was the high priest that year, said to them, 'You know nothing at all. Nor do you understand that it is better for you that one man should die for the people, not that the whole nation should perish.'"*

Soon it would be time for Jesus to finish His mission which included death. God used the religious leaders to fulfill prophecy. John 11:51-53 continues, *"He did not say this of his own accord, but being the high priest that year he prophesied that Jesus would die for the nation, and not for the nation only, but also to gather into one the children of God who are scattered abroad. So from that day on they made plans to put him to death."* It is humbling to realize that God does not just use the "super spiritual" to fulfill His work. He even used people who were against Him. God can even use a lost individual to prophesy for Him.

We read in the beginning in Mark 26:57 about Jesus being led to Caiaphas and the council. He had been arrested and knew what was coming in the day ahead. For some time now they have been trying to rally against him and levy charges. The High Council saw that their goal is now attainable. This is a great reminder that the crowd can be wrong.

Matthew 26:59-60 says, *"Now the chief priests and the whole council were seeking false testimony against Jesus that they might put him to death, but they found none, though many false witnesses came forward. At last two came forward."*

There were no charges to be brought against Jesus. Knowing this, they were seeking out those willing to lie about what Jesus had said or done. Not being able to do this, He spoke the truth as Jesus

DELIVERY PLAN DEVOTION 3

always does in verse 64, *"Jesus said to him, 'You have said so. But I tell you, from now on you will see the Son of Man seated at the right hand of Power and coming on the clouds of heaven.'"*

People are often offended and angry at the truth of the Gospel. We see a great example of this in verse 65 when the high priest tears his robe at what he feels is a blasphemous response. With this reaction to Jesus' words, a course is set in motion that leads Jesus to Pilate, and His eventual death and resurrection.

This anger at truth continues today in our culture. The Gospel should be offensive to those who argue so emphatically against it. We will eventually face this false witness to the message of Jesus from those who seek to discredit it. This is why it is so important that we equip ourselves to face it and address it with the same love and grace that the Lord shows us when we so obviously do not deserve it.

CAIAPHAS

DELIVERY PLAN, DEVOTION 4
Kyle Wendel // *Children & Student's Director*

Have you ever wondered how an evil man could be a part of God's plan? How can someone like that ever be used for the glory of God? One such person is recorded in John 11:45-53.

"Many of the Jews therefore, who had come with Mary and had seen what he did, believed in him, but some of them went to the Pharisees and told them what Jesus had done. So the chief priests and the Pharisees gathered the council and said, 'What are we to do? For this man performs many signs. If we let him go on like this, everyone will believe in him, and the Romans will come and take away both our place and our nation.' But one of them, Caiaphas, who was high priest that year, said to them, 'You know nothing at all. Nor do you understand that it is better for you that one man should die for the people, not that the whole nation should perish.' He did not say this of his own accord, but being high priest that year he prophesied that Jesus would die for the nation, and not for the nation only, but also to gather into one the children of God who are scattered abroad. So from that day on they made plans to put him to death."

Caiaphas was the High Priest at the time of Jesus' death. He was a Sadducee and a bitter enemy of Jesus. Caiaphas was one of the main advocates to plot to kill Jesus. After many people started to follow Jesus, the Pharisees had a meeting on trying to figure out what to do about Him. Jesus was stirring up all sorts of trouble for the Pharisees because the Gospel went against everything they were doing. The Pharisees had to figure out what to do about Jesus. Caiaphas had brought forth his plan to the group. He said it would be better for Jesus to die for the people than for the whole nation to perish. He was referring to the Romans possibly taking out the Jews. So, Caiaphas planned to kill Jesus to save the nation, but also because of the trouble Jesus was causing for the Pharisees.

DELIVERY PLAN DEVOTION 4

Later on in the story, we see Jesus was taken to the house of Caiaphas before He was taken to Pilate. There he most likely would have been questioned by the Sanhedrin and Pharisees before they decided to take Him to Pilate and ultimately decided to crucify Him.

We could wonder how Caiaphas could be a part of God's ultimate plan. However, Caiaphas was a part of the plan. God allowed Caiaphas to have a strong opposition to Jesus to ultimately fulfill the prophecies of Christ's death on the cross. There would have to be an opposition to Christ for the prophecy to be fulfilled.

We may wonder how we can learn something from Caiaphas today? I think we can take that sometimes we need to trust in God's plan and who He has allowed in positions of power. God had allowed Caiaphas to have his seat of power to orchestrate the ultimate plan of salvation. Today there are tons of people in power. We may not always like or believe in them, but we must remember God has allowed them to have that position and it can be part of a greater plan that we do not even know yet.

ROMAN SOLDIERS

DELIVERY PLAN, DEVOTION 5
Donna Fox // *Assistant to the Growth Pastor*

Mark 15:16-20 says, *"And the soldiers led him away inside the palace (that is, the governor's headquarters) and they called together the whole battalion. And they clothed him in a purple cloak, and twisting together a crown of thorns, they put it on him. And they began to salute him, 'Hail, King of the Jews!' And they were striking his head with a reed and spitting on him and kneeling down in homage to him. And when they had mocked him, they stripped him of the purple cloak and put his own clothes on him. And they led him out to crucify him."*

The Roman Soldiers delivered Jesus to His death. Pilate gave Jesus over to the crowd for crucifixion in place of Barabbas. The soldiers had their orders, "Crucify Him!"

They beat Him and tortured Him. They placed a crown of thorns on His head, mocked Him, nailed Him to the cross, and killed Him. Read Matthew 27:27-31. It describes the torture even further. He was stripped, thorns placed on His head, and reeds in His hand. He was mocked, spit on, and led away to be crucified. The Roman Soldiers were wicked men, enjoying their job a little too much, casting lots to see who would get His garments.

How would you like to have a job like that? After given the order to crucify, they carried out these horrific acts to the point of death. How could they do that to any man, much less the Son of God?

This was their job, to obey the orders and to crucify people. There was no emotional stake. The ones they crucified meant nothing to them. They did not realize who He was until after His death. Mark 15:39 says, *"And when the centurion, who stood facing him, saw that in this way he breathed his last, he said, 'Truly this man was the Son of God!'"* Here we see the Centurion, the head of the Roman Soldiers who realized the truth and was changed by Jesus.

DELIVERY PLAN DEVOTION 5

Why crucifixion? Crucifixion was a Roman death, not the Jewish custom which was stoning. Pontius Pilate gave the order. The Roman Soldiers simply carried it out.

The Roman Soldiers delivered Jesus to His death. They prepared Him by stripping Him and beating Him. They forced Him to carry His cross. They nailed Him to the boards. They tortured Him until He took His last breath. God had a plan when He sent Jesus to earth as a man. The crucifixion (and resurrection) was a fulfillment of that plan. Unknowingly, the Roman Soldiers had a part in that plan. They realized afterward what had just happened.

We are like the soldiers; our sin caused Jesus to be led to the cross to cover our sins.

BARABBAS

DELIVERY PLAN, DEVOTION 6
Debbie Kerr // *Office Administrator*

In 2004, Mel Gibson's blockbuster movie, The Passion of the Christ, opened in theaters all over the world. If you happened to be one of the few that did not see the film, go right now and watch it on Netflix or rent the DVD. It was an amazing, extremely graphic adaptation of the life of Jesus leading up to and including His crucifixion. The film grossed over $300 million dollars! Practically the whole world watched and cried through this heart-wrenching Gospel account. I cried throughout the movie like the rest of the sold out crowd in that theater, but the most powerful scene to me was the one where Jesus was sentenced to death. When Pontius Pilate asked who he should set free, the crowd went crazy yelling for the release of Barabbas. I watched Barabbas, the rebellious rioter and murderer sentenced to death, set free from his shackles and impending brutal death. He then ran out of Pilate's Hall yelling, "I'm free, I'm free!" Jesus took on Barabbas' shackles and was whipped, beaten, and dragged through the ridiculing crowd being led to His death. I was so overcome with intense emotion. The thought that I am Barabbas and had also been sentenced to death and set free, hit me fresh in the face and my heart. I had heard this account my entire life. I accepted Jesus as my Savior at the age of eleven and never strayed away from my faith. But at that moment, it was as if I was hearing it for the first time. I was more grateful than I had ever been. I was again reminded that this amazing transfer was indeed the most beautiful exchange.

Barabbas' story is a very important account in Scripture; this account is in all four Gospels. The name Barabbas can be broken down as "Bar" (son of) and "Abbas" (father) meaning "daddy" or "son of father." Jesus Christ is God's only begotten Son making Him the "Son of the Father." Barabbas was a notorious criminal, on death row. He was guilty of insurrection (rioting and rebelling) and murder because he had rebelled against the Roman Domination of that day. The time of Jesus' arrest came during the feast of the Passover. It was customary to release one prisoner during this holy

DELIVERY PLAN DEVOTION 6

feast. God in His infinite wisdom used real life examples to reveal His plan and how that plan included all mankind. You see, Barabbas represents all of us. Even if we never incited a rebellion or killed anyone, we are still born a complete sinner in need of a Savior. We read in Romans 3:23, **"For ALL have sinned and fall short of the glory of God."** Barabbas represented all of us! He was set free, and Jesus took his and our penalty. One of the interesting points here is that God set the vilest sinner in that day free so that we could also be set free. God can and will use whoever He wants to fulfill His plan. Barabbas' release or pardon, indicted Jesus, the sinless, spotless Lamb of God and sentenced Him to a cruel, horrific, death on the cross.

Scripture does not reveal what happened to Barabbas after he was set free, his supporting role in the story was finished. He fulfilled the purpose God had planned for him. He won the lottery that day, but did he win it for all eternity? Scripture does not reveal whether Barabbas put his faith in the One who took his place. Chances are he did not, or it most likely would have been included in the Gospel story.

How about you? Have you put your faith in the One who took your place?

Trading Your life, For my offenses
For my redemption, You carried all the blame
Breaking the curse, Of our condition
Perfection took our place
When only love
Could make a way
You gave Your life
In a beautiful exchange
(Lyrics from *The Beautiful Exchange* by Hillsong)

DELIVERY PLAN DEVOTION 6

05
DELIVERY DAY

CAROLE COMBS,
WIFE OF LEAD PASTOR JIM COMBS

DELIVERY DAY WEEK 5

I was excited to see the package delivery truck drive up my driveway. As the delivery person walked to my front door, I was wondering why I may be receiving a package as I did not remember ordering anything. I opened the front door and stepped out onto the front porch to receive the package. Sadly, the package was addressed to my youngest son. Obviously, he had ordered something and had it delivered to my address. With a little disappointment, I signed for the package. I guess if I did not order anything why would I be excited or expecting a delivery?

I do not know why but there is something exciting to me about getting a delivery. As I began to step towards my front door to go back inside my house, the delivery person began to scold me for not having a visible house address. I told him that I knew this and that I was sorry. It was not over then, he then asked me why it was not at the end of my driveway near the road. I told him that it had been at one time, but the snow plow trucks had broken it and knocked it down in the winter, and we had never replaced it. The conversation continued. He then began to tell me where I should put the address on my house (I am sorry to all delivery personnel for making your job more difficult).

If an expected package came to your home and it was addressed to you, what would you do with the package?

_____
_____
_____

The package was not for me that day, but one day I am expecting a package delivery. It is a delivery beyond this world! This package has already been signed for and paid. This package is a gift especially for me. However, this package can be delivered to you as well at no cost to you. Now, this may sound too good to be true and somewhat like an infomercial. Please read on!

DELIVERY DAY WEEK 5

God came into this world in the form of mankind all packaged up. He came as a special delivery, a baby boy that was born in Bethlehem to a virgin mother named Mary. **"Behold, the virgin shall conceive and bear a son, and they shall call his name Immanuel (which means, God with us)"** (Matthew 1:23 and Isaiah 7:14). **"She will bear a son, and you shall call his name Jesus, for he will save his people from their sins"** (Matthew 1:21). Jesus came to deliver you and me from our sins. The delivery that I am personally expecting is the delivery of my soul. I do not know when that will be, but I will be leaving this temporary home called earth and will be transported to my eternal home called Heaven. This delivery of my soul is not a pipe-dream. My soul will be delivered to the very presence of my Lord and Savior Jesus Christ who dwells in the heavens with the Father. I will not receive this deliverance based on something I have done, earned, or even bought. Romans 3:10-12 says, **"As it is written: 'None is righteous, no, not one; no one understands; no one seeks for God. All have turned aside; together they have become worthless; no one does good, not even one.'"** My sin separated me from a holy God. **"Then desire when it has conceived gives birth to sin, and sin when it is fully grown brings forth death"** (James 1:15).

I needed to be delivered from death. This is not a physical death because our mortal bodies will die. This death is a spiritual death, a separation from God for all of eternity. **"But God shows his love for us in that while we were still sinners, Christ died for us. Since, therefore, we have now been justified by his blood, much more shall we be saved by him from the wrath of God"** (Romans 5:8-9).

DELIVERY DAY WEEK 5

Have you been delivered from death? Explain how you know that you have been delivered (If you are not sure that you have been delivered, please speak to your Pastor or your Growth Community leader without delay).

_____
_____
_____

I was twelve years old when I realized that my sins were against a holy and righteous God. These sins separated me from God for all eternity if I was not willing to trust God's Son Jesus as my Savior. Christ died on the cross to pay the penalty for sin, which is death and by the way, it is the penalty for your sin as well. God's love is so great that there is no sin too big or too small that He will not forgive. Do not limit God in His greatness to forgive your sins. This is the same God who painted the skies blue, and created the highest mountains to the lowest valleys and everywhere in between. We are the ones who limit God! The package of salvation has been delivered to you and me to receive. It has been paid for by the blood of Jesus on the cross. The Bible says, **"Because, if you confess with your mouth that Jesus is Lord and believe in your heart that God raised him from the dead, you will be saved. For with the heart one believes and is justified, and with the mouth one confesses and is saved. For everyone who calls on the name of the Lord will be saved'"** (Romans 10:9-10,13).

Anthony Ray Hinton was one of the longest-serving death row prisoners in Alabama's history and among the longest-serving condemned prisoners to be freed. He was exonerated from death after thirty years. I cannot even begin to imagine the thoughts going through Mr. Hinton's mind when he was exonerated from his death sentence. He was set free! He no longer had to live a life of imprisonment. With all due respect to Mr. Hinton, are you living a

DELIVERY DAY WEEK 5

life like Mr. Hinton before he was exonerated? Do the things of this world have you imprisoned?

What kind of things of this world imprison us?
_____
_____
_____

How can the things of this world imprison us?
_____
_____
_____

"Wretched man that I am! Who will deliver me from this body of death? Thanks be to God through Jesus Christ our Lord! So then, I myself serve the law of God with my mind, but with my flesh I serve the law of sin" (Romans 7:24-25). Jesus exonerated you and me. Mr. Hinton did not choose to stay imprisoned after being exonerated. He gladly received his release from prison. Open the package that has been delivered to you! Be delivered from the death sentence. Accept Jesus into your life today. Right now, right where you are. He is ready to set you free! You may have already trusted Christ as your Savior. You may have been delivered from death. You have received the delivery but have tossed aside what God has for your life of freedom.

What does it mean for a Christian to stay imprisoned?
_____
_____
_____

DELIVERY DAY WEEK 5

We have been exonerated from the penalty of sin when you and I have trusted Christ as our Savior. Why do you think sometimes believers live as if they are still imprisoned to sin? Do you live this way at times?

_____
_____
_____

Jesus said, **"I came that they may have life and have it abundantly"** (John 10:10b). I have heard from many people through the years that they do not read the Bible because they do not understand it. A responsibility of those that have been delivered from death is to learn and live like their Savior. What would happen if your employer gave you a new project at work that was expected to be completed by you correctly and with a deadline? You were very unfamiliar with this project that was assigned to you. Therefore, you opened the manual that your employer delivered to you along with the project assignment. The manual became difficult to read and became somewhat frustrating. So, you attempted the project without directions and with limited understanding. The day that your employer returns to you for the completed project might have some interesting results for you.

How would you describe this abundant life that Jesus speaks about in John 10:10?

_____
_____
_____

Do you think it is important for Christians to behave like and reflect Christ? Why? How could this be possible to do?

_____
_____
_____

99

DELIVERY DAY WEEK 5

What could be some possible repercussions of an employee not completing or partially completing a project that had been assigned to them by their employer?

_____
_____
_____

God is not going to remove any of His children from being His children. The Bible tells us that when we accept Christ as our Savior, that is for all eternity (John 10:28-29) However, you will miss the life that was meant for you. It is a life that will bring God glory. We are all a project in the process. I am so glad that God loves projects. I know in this life, I will never remotely come close to repaying the Lord for what He did for me on the cross and neither will you. We are indebted. We need to live with purpose and on purpose reflecting who He is. *"He himself bore our sins in his body on the tree, that we might die to sin and live to righteousness. By his wounds you have been healed"* (1 Peter 2:24).

God's Word is our project manual. Here is a very small portion of Scripture that teaches you and me how we can live after being delivered from death. Let love be genuine. *"Let love be genuine. Abhor what is evil; hold fast to what is good. Love one another with brotherly affection. Outdo one another in showing honor. Do not be slothful in zeal, be fervent in spirit, serve the Lord. Rejoice in hope, be patient in tribulation, be constant in prayer. Contribute to the needs of the saints and seek to show hospitality"* (Romans 12:9-13).

What are some of the things listed for believers to do?

_____
_____
_____

DELIVERY DAY WEEK 5

How would you rate your Bible reading time? (10 was great and 1 was poor.)

_____
_____
_____

What excuses have you made for not getting into God's Word on a regular basis?

_____
_____
_____

I had a package arrive all the way from China. When the pair of boots I had ordered arrived, they were packaged in the original shoe box. The package was so crushed on the outside that I was concerned about the contents inside. I opened the package to find the boots that were in the box were still in perfect condition. Jesus was sent to this world for people, just like you and I. He was rejected and despised by this world. He was crushed for your sins and mine (Isaiah 53:3-5). The devil thought that he had crushed Jesus. He feared that Jesus would accomplish what He came to earth to do. Yes, Jesus did accomplish the Father's will for His life. Jesus had victory over death, hell, and the grave (Colossians 2:13-15). Satan is still at work today. You are not immune to his attacks. He fears that you might accomplish what you were meant to do on this earth. You were meant to live an abundant life, a life that is pleasing to God, and spend all of eternity with Him.

What thoughts are invoked when you hear about Jesus being crushed for your sins?

_____
_____
_____

DELIVERY DAY WEEK 5

Jesus has a special delivery for you, and he does not need your address. He knows where you live. Matter of fact, He knows everything about you. He does not want to scold you. He loves you and wants to deliver His mercy and grace to your life right where you are. This special delivery is His salvation. Jesus is knocking. Will you open the door of your heart and step out and receive him into your life? Will you be delivered from death? If you know that you have been delivered from death, are you allowing Satan to bring his destruction into your life, into your home? **"Little children, you are from God and have overcome them, for he who is in you is greater than he who is in the world"** (1 John 4:4). We are the victors through Jesus Christ our Lord. You do not have to live a defeated life. You have been exonerated! Praise God! Get into God's Word, the Bible. Learn and take the truth from God's Word. Satan disguises truth with lies, right with wrongs, and love with hate. He wants to dull your capacity to hear and see God. Satan wants you to be comfortable with sin and to trivialize it.

What lies are you believing? How has Satan disguised himself to you?

_____
_____
_____

DELIVERY DAY WEEK 5

I would like to share a portion of a song I learned as a little girl. I could not stop thinking of it as I wrote about how our lives can be delivered from death.

What can wash away my sin?
Nothing but the blood of Jesus
What can make me whole again?
Nothing but the blood of Jesus
Nothing can my sin erase
Nothing but the blood the Jesus
Naught of works, tis all of grace
Nothing but the blood of Jesus
This is all my hope and peace
Nothing but the blood of Jesus
This is all my righteousness
Nothing but the blood of Jesus

I am signed, sealed, and delivered! What about you?

DELIVERY DAY WEEK 5

THE RESURRECTION

DELIVERY DAY, DEVOTION 1

Jill Osmon // *Assistant to the Lead Pastor*

"**He is not here, but has risen. Remember how he told you, while he was still in Galilee, that the Son of Man must be delivered into the hands of sinful men and be crucified and on the third day rise.**" Luke 24:6-7

Growing up in church, Easter was always a big deal. We always got new outfits, always looked really nice that Sunday, and the chocolate bunny was always an added bonus! I knew it was more than all of those things, but as a kid, who self-admittedly was very sheltered, the depth of what Easter was did not land in my mind.

As an adult, the weight of what Easter is, what we celebrate and recognize, should be humbling, it should be something that gives us hope and joy while understanding the sacrifice. Unfortunately, I find myself focusing on everything but that. I worry about events, about family, about clothes, and a slew of other well-intentioned things that are not important when compared to the resurrection. I am sure you have things that you focus on during this time of year that seem less important when you begin to remember what we celebrate this time of year. So I guess what I should say is what Easter should mean to me, how should Easter shape how I live my life.

Because of the foundational importance of the death, burial, and resurrection of Jesus, I think we sometimes complicate it more than it is. Josh McDowell says it best, "Few people seem to realize that the resurrection of Jesus is the cornerstone to a worldview that provides the perspective to all of life." Everything that we do should be through the purview of the resurrection. Acts 4:33 says, *"And with great power the apostles were giving their testimony to the resurrection of the Lord Jesus, and great grace was upon them all."* God will give us grace; He will give us strength and hope and joy, all that we need to live a life that brings Him glory.

DELIVERY DAY DEVOTION 1

I am a pretty steady person; not much can knock me off the course I believe God has for me. I am not easily swayed, not easily emotionally manipulated, and not much can unsteady me. I wish I could say that steadiness is always based on the foundation of God and His goodness, but a lot of the time it is based on my strength, my work, and that fails 100% of the time. Charles Stanley says, "There is only one secure foundation: a genuine, deep relationship with Jesus Christ, which will carry you through any and all turmoil. No matter what storms are raging all around, you'll stand firm if you stand on His love."

That is what Easter means to me; it is that which I strive to have my life completely and assuredly attached. The resurrection, it is where our hope and joy comes from because without the resurrection our faith has no foundation. I love this quote, "No matter how devastating our struggles, disappointments, and troubles are, they are only temporary. No matter what happens to you, no matter the depth of tragedy or pain you face, no matter how death stalks you and your loved ones, the Resurrection promises you a future of immeasurable good" (Josh McDowell).

This year let us challenge ourselves to realign where our foundation lies, that our hope and our joy comes from the one place that can always promise immeasurable goodness, that is Jesus.

HE IS NOT HERE

DELIVERY DAY, DEVOTION 2
Ryan Story // *Student Pastor*

When I was a child, Easter was nothing more than getting some candy. When I became a teenager, Easter was nothing more than getting a few days off of school. When I was in my twenties, I was working at a grocery store; Easter was nothing more than a week where I could get some overtime. Easter did not start to mean something to me until Jesus started to mean something to me. All my life I believed I would become my surroundings. My surroundings involved drinking, drugs, depression, anger, doubt, sadness, passive aggressiveness, neglect, chaos, and darkness. That is where I was going to be my whole life, but Easter changed that.

One of my favorite Easter verses in the Bible is only four simple words. If I wanted to embrace the contraction, it would be three simple words. Matthew 28:6 says, *"He is not here."* An angel said that to both ladies named Mary when they went to visit the tomb where Jesus was buried. They expected to see what they saw the day before, a tomb filled with a loved one. The ladies never thought that view would change. Mary knew that her Son was buried and died, and she had accepted that as a reality. The hurt of being alone with no husband and now no son must have been heart-wrenching. Mary Magdalene went to see a man who loved her, taught her, and helped teach her about godly things. Now only hurt remained and that became her new reality. Before those two got to the tomb, I wish I could have been there as they woke up that morning to go to the tomb. Each woman was passing each other with those weak smiles that we show when we are destroyed on the inside. As they walked and got closer to the tomb, I am sure anger, doubt, and sadness started taking over their lives. But then they saw the tomb was open, and they were told the four greatest words recorded in the Bible, *"He is not here."*

That means so much to me because at one point I never thought life could be any different. I was born into a family with a drinking

DELIVERY DAY DEVOTION 2

problem, which meant my kids would be born into a family that had a drinking problem. I lived in darkness as a kid that means I would always live in darkness. When I looked at my life, I was always going to be "here," inside that tomb. I would never get out of "here." "Here" in my life was the pit of sin and the hurt I encountered. Easter means the world to me because Jesus rose from the tomb so I could leave mine. Since Jesus was not "here," that meant that I did not have to be or stay in my "here." It is one of those sobering feelings to look back at where life used to be. I think back to being in a place of such darkness, and because of Jesus I did not have to stay there. Because He left, that meant I did not have to stay there. That is what Easter means to me.

VICTORY

DELIVERY DAY, DEVOTION 3
Philip Piasecki // *Worship Leader*

I have never liked to lose. I feel like that is pretty common in most men, we just do not like to lose. Most of the time, I can be a gracious loser, but sometimes I am not able to hold in my disappointment. My brother and I both had so many battles growing up where inevitably one of us would end up angry because we lost. If we are honest, it was him (being the younger brother) who lost more than he won, but he occasionally beat me. There is nothing like the feeling of victory and nothing like the disappointment of defeat.

When I was asked to write about what Easter means to me, the first word that came to mind was "Victory." As someone who does not like to lose, the idea of victory pumps me up. It is so easy to be beaten down by the world, sometimes to feel like the devil is winning. Easter is a yearly reminder that Jesus won. It is sad how easily believers can forget about the victory we have in Jesus Christ. So many of us live our lives with such a miserable outlook, dreading each day instead of celebrating it. When we remember what Christ did for us on the cross, and we understand that we are children of God, our attitude will change drastically. Each Sunday as we gather as the church, we should be reminded of this, and it is especially true on Easter.

Romans 8:11 says, **"If the Spirit of him who raised Jesus from the dead dwells in you, he who raised Christ Jesus from the dead will also give life to your mortal bodies through his Spirit who dwells in you."**

This verse is so encouraging to believers. Jesus rose from the dead, and His Spirit lives in us and gives us life. Easter reinvigorates the truth of that Scripture in my life every year. We get to come together as the Church on Resurrection Sunday and proclaim that truth together as the body of Christ. When I think of Easter, I think of victory. Jesus conquered death, hell, and the grave. He was raised up so that we would be able to spend eternity with Him. Whenever you are feeling discouraged, remember Jesus' victory.

DELIVERY DAY DEVOTION 3

CELEBRATE

DELIVERY DAY, DEVOTION 4
Noble Baird // *Community Center Director*

Easter has always been an exciting time of year for me. When I was younger, I will never forget waking up in the morning and to search all over the house to find the eggs my parents had hidden. As I became older, Easter took on a more meaningful and special time. I started to understand the true meaning of Easter and how it was not all about the eggs, the candy, and toys that would be hidden around the house. Instead, Easter has become a time of remembrance, but more importantly a celebration!

In 1 Corinthians 15, Paul gives the first written account of the resurrection of Christ. Within this passage, he lays out the foundational truths for which our faith stands. Starting in 1 Corinthians 15:1-4, he writes, **"Now I would remind you, brothers, of the gospel I preached to you, which you received, in which you stand, and by which you are being saved, if you hold fast to the word I preached to you—unless you believed in vain. For I delivered to you as of first importance what I also received: that Christ died for our sins in accordance with the Scriptures, that he was buried, that he was raised on the third day in accordance with the Scriptures."** These three truths are pointed out by Paul: Christ's death, Christ's burial, and Christ's resurrection. It is within these three declarations that we have the Gospel by which our sins are cleared.

One of my absolute favorite worship songs is "Resurrecting" by Elevation Church. It is truly a beautiful song, proclaiming the message of these foundational pillars in 1 Corinthians 15. This is the final verse in the song:

"The tomb where soldiers watched in vain
Was borrowed for three days
His body there would not remain
Our God has robbed the grave
Our God has robbed the grave."

DELIVERY DAY DEVOTION 4

I love this verse because that is exactly what happened when Christ walked out of that tomb. The soldiers were wasting their time, Christ was simply borrowing Joseph's tomb, and then he robbed Satan of what he thought was his greatest victory. So, as we continue in this Easter season, let us never forget that empty tomb that was only borrowed, as we celebrate the victory that Christ won for us!

SPECIAL OCCASIONS WITH GRANDMA EDDIE

DELIVERY DAY, DEVOTION 5
Richie Henson // *Production Director*

I was privileged growing up to be raised by godly people. Both of my parents loved Jesus and gave their lives to the Lord through the church in full-time ministry. Beyond my parents, I spent a great deal of my time with my Grandma Eddie. She was truly one of the kindest and godliest people I have ever known.

My Grandma Eddie loved to cook for her family and holidays were a wonderfully special time. One of the biggest holidays at Grandma Eddie's house was Easter. She would cook ham, turkey, thirty-seven sides and fourteen pies. Not to mention all the Easter cookies and candy. To say the least, it was a huge celebration that I look back on fondly.

In 2010, while on a trip to Yosemite National Park with the sixth-grade class I was teaching, I received news that my dear Grandma Eddie had passed away. It was, and on certain occasions still is a difficult truth for me. I was so very close to her, and the loss of her love and joy in this world can be heartbreaking. However, I make sure to never relinquish her memory. I try on all occasions to tell my son how wonderful and godly his great-grandmother was.

I am especially reminded of my grandma at Easter. Many of my family members including my wife have taken up the mantle of making Easter special by recreating Grandma Eddie's famous sugar cookies. Every time I eat one of these cookies, I am reminded of the pain of losing her, but with each savory bite, I am also reminded that Easter is a time to celebrate the realities of salvation.

My grandma spent many years of her life struggling with pain and difficulty. She survived breast cancer twice and lived many years with diabetes. Nonetheless, today, she is in Heaven, devoid of pain and instead filled with joy and the fulfillment of meeting her Jesus just as it says in Revelation 21:4, **"He will wipe away every tear from their eyes, and death shall be no more, neither shall**

DELIVERY DAY DEVOTION 5

there be mourning, nor crying, nor pain anymore, for the former things have passed away."

Easter is such a special occasion where we can all celebrate the resurrection of Jesus in expectation of the fulfillment of our salvation when one day we are taken to be home in Heaven. I cannot wait for the day when I get to see Grandma Eddie again, and we both can sing our praises to Jesus thanking Him for the resurrection that makes Easter so sweet.

G.R.A.C.E.

DELIVERY DAY, DEVOTION 6
Wes McCullough // Production Director

In the spring of 2004, a movie was released that rocked the world. It was bloody and violent, but people still flocked to see the rated R film. The premise of the movie was the brutal death of one man. Watching this film caused masses of people to weep and make life changes. The movie was *THE PASSION OF THE CHRIST*.

Having grown up knowing the story of Jesus' death, the movie was not as much a surprise as it was a reminder and a visualization of His sacrifice. I do not watch the movie every year, but I am reminded of it each year through the Easter season. Memotries of the graphic visuals flood my memory, and I am humbled knowing Jesus accepted that fate in my place. I have fallen short of His glory, but God's grace is abundant.

The theme of Easter 2015 at The River Church (Holly) was "Undefeated." There was a boxing ring on stage as a visual for Christ's battle with Satan. You and I were destined for a fight with Satan that we could not win. It was going to be an excruciating, torturous beating for the rest of eternity. When Jesus died, He stepped into that ring to fight Satan in our place. Christ's victory in that battle was unquestionable. Jesus gave us victory over death and punishment.

1 Peter 2:24 says it all, *"He himself bore our sins in his body on the tree, that we might die to sin and live to righteousness. By his wounds you have been healed."*

Isaiah 53:5 is similarly a favorite, *"But he was pierced for our transgressions; he was crushed for our iniquities; upon him was the chastisement that brought us peace, and with his wounds we are healed."*

These verses are a reminder of the punishment Christ took on our behalf. We have all sinned and been separated from God, but Jesus

DELIVERY DAY DEVOTION 6

paid the price to reunite us with our Heavenly Father. *"For by grace you have been saved through faith. And this is not your own doing; it is the gift of God"* (Ephesians 2:8).

If it helps, remember grace this way:
G- God's
R- Riches
A- At
C- Christ's
E- Expense

This Easter season do not be distracted by the commercialized Easter bunny, eggs, and candy. Focus on the victory you have been given and thank Jesus for fighting for you.

OUR MISSION

Matthew 28:19-20: *"Go therefore and make disciples of all nations, baptizing them in the name of the Father and of the Son and of the Holy Spirit, teaching them to observe all that I have commanded you. And behold, I am with you always, to the end of the age."*

REACH

At The River Church, you will often hear the phrase, "we don't go to church, we are the Church." We believe that as God's people, our primary purpose and goal is to go out and make disciples of Jesus Christ. We encourage you to reach the world in your local communities.

GATHER

Weekend Gatherings at The River Church are all about Jesus, through singing, giving, serving, baptizing, taking the Lord's Supper, and participating in messages that are all about Jesus and bringing glory to Him. We know that when followers of Christ gather together in unity, it's not only a refresher it's bringing life-change.

GROW

Our Growth Communities are designed to mirror the early church in Acts as having "all things in common." They are smaller collections of believers who spend time together studying the word, knowing and caring for one another relationally, and learning to increase their commitment to Christ by holding one another accountable.

The River Church
8393 E. Holly Rd. Holly, MI 48442
theriverchurch.cc • info@theriverchurch.cc

BOOKS BY THE RIVER CHURCH

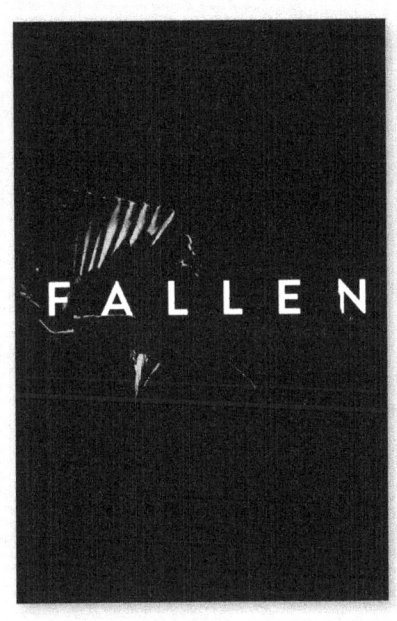

Johnny Be Good
THE LEGACY OF JOHN THE BAPTIST

FALLEN

FRIGHTFUL
WHEN CHRISTMAS BECAME DELIGHTFUL

THE FAMILY TREE
GROWING A GODLY FAMILY

Made in the USA
Columbia, SC
19 January 2018